Commemorating Epimetheus

Philosophy/Communication
Ramsey Eric Ramsey, Series Editor

Commemorating Epimetheus

By Les Amis

Translated by S. Pluháček

Purdue University Press
West Lafayette, Indiana

Amis, Les.
 Commemorating Epimetheus / by Les Amis ; translated by S.
Pluháček.
    p. cm.
 Includes bibliographical references and index.
 ISBN 978-1-55753-497-2 (alk. paper)
 1. Sharing. 2. Conduct of life. I. Pluháček, Stephen. II. Title.
 BJ1533.G4A55 2008
 177'.7--dc22

                        2008034084

Contents

Commemorating Epimetheus

. . . sharing all with all. In this way the abundance of the earth grew, bringing forth again and again that circle of birth and death through which all were provided with a share of elemental abundance.

. . . sharing all with all, the overflowing abundance of the earth was in no way diminished. Indeed, through such sharing abundance was shared forth again and again.

Season followed upon season, and nothing died forever. Again and again the earth shared forth myriad things. And light followed upon dark, the warm upon the cold, the moist upon the dry, and life followed upon death. Each shared with each, coming together and pulling apart harmoniously, benefiting and enhancing all without sacrifice. Each shared with each, the knot of existence so firmly tied together in and through this sharing that none stood apart from the others. And yet, there was no fusion in all of this—with all fused in a sameness without distinction. Rather, there was harmony—harmony, in which neither one nor the other was suppressed or annulled.

. . . a sea flowing and rushing upon itself, a ring circling back upon itself. . .

Sharing: the swaying movement of all that is.

Scarcity, and its offspring avarice and poverty, had not yet been seen upon the earth. The overflowing abundance of the earth was shared by all. And because there was always more than enough, there was no need, no desire to arrest the sharing, to close it off from others, to appropriate it as one's own. Each sharing with each, there was not yet anything proper to one alone. Mutually uplifting and reinforcing one another, there was no greed or jealousy upon the earth. Nothing was held back, nothing held in reserve. There was thus not yet expenditure nor return. That circle had not yet come to be.

◆ ◆ ◆

When mortal creatures lived with the gods, the powers of the earth were still strong. Elemental energy ebbed and flowed. There was not yet any sacrifice. For who would sacrifice to whom? And what was there to sacrifice? There being everything in abundance, each sharing all with all, the world itself was a temple, all places altars, every event a sacrament.

◆ ◆ ◆

It began in wonder—a wonder that it began at all.

One day Wonder unexpectedly brought forth from out of herself twins, each joined to the other. Later, these twins came to be named Awe and Anticipation. Awe, forever lingering in the moment, greeted all that came her way with an open heart filled with gratitude. Anticipation, forever looking away, greeted all that came her way with a heart opened like a flower greeting the rising sun. One day, it happened that these twins set out along separate paths, with Awe walking along the way of wakefulness and Anticipation walking along the way of awakening. Now and then, their paths would cross, but it happened that neither could look the other in the face.

It was long ago forgotten whose progeny Wonder is; she precedes even the ancestral gods.

◆ ◆ ◆

Along the way, Epimetheus came to live with the all-sharing Earth in order to learn from her. He was at that time without name. But sharing in her commemoration of life and death, again and again sharing in her bringing-forth of life out of death and death out of life, he came to partake in her fluid and creative wisdom of unfolding the vital energies of incipient tendency and immanent renewal. Following the ways of the Earth, commemorating her ways by participating in the sharing forth of all that is, he came to be known as Epimetheus, he who thinks after. For by learning from the Earth, he was said to think after her ways. And by sharing in the commemoration of life and death, by sharing in the memory of what has been and yet still opens and unfolds the present and future, he was said to think after the past so as to care for the present and the future. In this way, Epimetheus remained open and receptive to the claims of all that was brought forth.

One day, as Epimetheus was following the ways of the Earth, his heart opened, and the pain and suffering of the earth flooded in. For Epimetheus there was a joy even in this pain and suffering.

Along the way, Prometheus also came to live with the all-sharing Earth. He was in the beginning without name. Unlike Epimetheus, Prometheus did not partake in the commemoration of life and death. Although he himself had come to be from out of the abundance of all that is and never suffered from want of anything, he found himself plagued by a fear that one day that which had never happened might happen: that the all-sharing Earth would cease to bring forth ever and again abundance out of abundance. He was the first who thought it both desirable and possible to live without faith—that is, without sharing in that sharing-forth of all-that-is through which all that is needed is brought forth ever and again. He believed that it was necessary to prepare for a time without abundance—not because such a time was unavoidable, but simply out of folly. Thus he came to be known as Prometheus, he who thinks before. For by laying up provisions while surrounded by abundance, he was said to think before he looked around. Failing to see that only by sharing would abundance continue to be shared forth, Prometheus set about closing off from others and appropriating as his own that which can only be shared. Despite Prometheus' lack of faith, the all-sharing Earth continued to hold nothing back, letting Prometheus be in his folly. For this too was a part of the Earth's abundance.

From out of Prometheus' folly a fear of death was born. Folly upon folly. Before this time such fear had never shown its face upon the earth. And shamefully (for thus too was shame born), this fear was a selfish fear—for it was not a fear for others, for the death of others, but a fear of one's own death that showed its face. This fear of death, of "one's own death," spread over humankind, blanketing in oblivion the commemoration of sharing with others in life and death.

Epimetheus was not one to sacrifice the flower of the present moment. Rising with the sun, each morning he would bathe in cool waters, renewing and refreshing himself. Often he would then spend his days sitting amidst tall trees, wrapped in reverie, contemplating the miracle of every moment. In undisturbed silence and solitude, he was never bothered by the lapse of time. Thus Epimetheus' days were not days of some week, nor were they broken up into hours and minutes to be counted by some artifice. Embracing each moment with wonder, he sacrificed to no heathen deity.

It has been said that Epimetheus, wise before all others, and Prometheus, clever above all others, were descended from Awe and Anticipation, and that, like Awe and Anticipation, there was a time when they too were joined to one another, walking over the earth together.

◆ ◆ ◆

Later, long after all of this had been forgotten, plowed under and covered over, it was said that at one time there had been no mortal creatures, and that only the gods existed. And that when the time came for mortal creatures to be brought forth, the gods fashioned them out of earth and fire and various compounds of both elements in the interior of the earth. When these creatures were about to be brought forth into the light of day, Prometheus and Epimetheus were asked to bestow upon them suitable powers and abilities. Epimetheus said to Prometheus: "I am the more experienced. Let me bestow, and you study my work." This was agreed, and Epimetheus set about his task. He clothed them with thick hair and tough skins sufficient to insulate them against the winter cold and able to resist the summer heat, and serving also as a natural bed of their own when they wanted to rest. He also shod them, furnishing them with hoofs and hair and hard and callous skins under their feet. Out of the earth's abundance, he provided them all with suitable food—plants of the soil to some, to others fruits from trees, and to others roots. And to some he gave other animals as food. And some he made to have few young ones, whereas those who were their prey were very prolific, and in this manner their survival was ensured. And when he had protected them against hunger and the changing seasons, he set about providing them with various ways of avoiding mutual destruction. There were some upon whom he bestowed strength without swiftness, whereas he conferred swiftness upon those who were weaker. Some he armed, and others he left unarmed, but devised for them some other means of preservation, making some large and having their size as a protection, and others small, whose nature was to fly in the air or burrow in the ground, this being their way of escape. In this way he harmoniously shared out powers and abilities, providing each of them with a suitable manner of living, and seeing to it that no race would become extinct. Thus Epimetheus, whom some have thought not very wise, bestowed upon the animals the various powers and abilities he thought suitable—and when he came to human beings, he paused in wonder. Now while Epimetheus was marveling at humankind, Prometheus came to study what his brother had done. He understood how the other animals had been taken care of, but when he saw that humans were naked and shoeless, and had neither bed nor arms of defense, Prometheus became perplexed and agitated. The appointed hour was approaching when humans were to be brought forth into the light of day; and Prometheus, not knowing how they might survive, entered by stealth the common workshop in which Athena and Hephaestus practiced their arts, stole the practical arts together with fire (for the practical arts could have been neither acquired nor used without fire), and forced them upon humans. In the beginning, Prometheus' machinations were met with a certain astonishment. Only later were the ill-gotten gains of the crooked schemer thoughtlessly accepted. In this way human beings were made clever through Prometheus, but lost that wisdom bestowed by Epimetheus. Some have said that Prometheus was later prosecuted for theft, owing to the blunder of Epimetheus. But others tell a different story.

Humans, having then a share of certain divine attributes on account of Prometheus' theft, were the only animals who entered into commerce with the gods. Humans alone were bound to the gods, raising altars and sacred images. They soon learned to speak and to name, as well as to make houses, clothes, shoes, and beds, and to draw sustenance from the earth. Thus provided, humankind at first lived dispersed, and there were no cities. But as a result of this dispersal they were destroyed by the wild beasts for they were utterly weak in comparison to them, and although their art was sufficient to provide them with nourishment, it did not help them when fighting with other animals. Food they had, but not yet the art of politics, of which the art of war is said to be a part. After a while a strange desire for self-preservation drove them toward one another. But when they had been driven together, having no art of politics, they wronged one another and were again in process of dispersion and destruction. Thinking that humankind was in need of some kind of political art, Prometheus set off to steal this as well. But such knowledge was in the keeping of Zeus, and the power of Prometheus did not extend to entering into the citadel of heaven, where Zeus, who had terrifying sentinels, dwelt. Zeus, like Prometheus, feared that the entire human race would be exterminated, and so he sent Hermes to them, bearing reverence and justice to be the ordering principles of cities and the bonds of friendship and conciliation. Hermes asked Zeus how he should distribute justice and reverence among humans. Should he distribute them as the other arts are distributed; that is to say, to a favored few only, one skilled person having enough of medicine or of any other art for many unskilled ones? "Shall this be the manner in which I am to distribute justice and reverence among humans, or shall I give them to all?" "To all," said Zeus; "I should like them all to have a share. For cities cannot exist if only a few share in the virtues, as is the case in the other arts. And further, make a law by my order that anyone who has no part in reverence and justice shall be put to death, for such a person is a plague to the state."

And this is said to be the reason why humankind in general, when the question relates to carpentering or any other mechanical art, allow only a few to share in their deliberations, and when anyone else interferes, they object, if this person is not of the favored few, which is very natural. But when they meet to deliberate about political excellence, which proceeds only by way of justice and wisdom, they are patient enough of any person who speaks of them, as is also natural, because they think that everyone ought to share in this sort of virtue, and that states could not exist if this were otherwise.

Now, in addition to theft, Prometheus was known to stray from the truth. And this story, like so many others, comes from Prometheus. Yet this story too has a share in the truth—even if it would substitute merely one part for that of all others. There is, of course, a price to pay for this Promethean substitution: in always looking forward, humans have neglected the commemoration of the past, burying it in forgetfulness. Even so, the commemoration of the past has not been altogether abandoned. Here and there some have devoted themselves to carrying the past forward. Here and there some recall that long ago, before Epimetheus and Prometheus were regarded as gods, they walked upon the earth as humans among humans.

◆ ◆ ◆

Before the gods, men and women were exposed and entrusted to one another. Abiding with one another, there was neither host nor guest. Nor was one the hostage of another. No one stood above any other. They walked the earth together, hand in hand. And in this way, they shared in the commemoration of all-that-is. There was not then the giving and taking, the giving and receiving that would later come to stand between humans as well as between humans and the gods. Words had not yet been brought forth, casting rainbows and illusive bridges between things forever apart. Nor had any sacrifice been offered, casting rainbows and illusive bridges between things forever as one. Rather, each shared with each in the swaying movement of creation.

◆ ◆ ◆

Epimetheus was once heard to ask, "If Prometheus had such great foresight, why did all his machinations, all his ruses turn out so badly?"

Some friends of Epimetheus were once heard to say, "That Prometheus is quite a trickster. He goes about bringing trouble to others, yet gets away without bearing the burden of his transgressions."

"Yes, but let us not forget the punishment meted out to him by Zeus. Did he not suffer greatly for overstepping the boundaries set before him?"

"Perhaps. But let us not forget the praise and adulation he has received for all his suffering. Has he not become like a god to those he hurt? Have not his poisoned gifts been received without the least suspicion?"

"Yes, what is all this clamoring and praise about reverence and justice among humans? They strut about all puffed up with pride, unaware of all they have lost through Prometheus' theft of fire and the practical arts. It was his theft that called forth the need for reverence and justice. And they are but poor substitutes for what our friend Epimetheus has shared with humans."

"Yes, Prometheus is a master at giving with one hand while taking with the other. Those poor humans fail to appreciate the price they have paid for their supposed self-sufficiency. Why, they are unaware of their loss. That wonder shared out by our friend Epimetheus has been lost to them. They no longer tremble with awe before the mystery of all-that-is. They no longer stand with awe before the mystery of others. The poor fools, they fail to see that reverence and justice are but poor substitutes for the awe that Epimetheus awakened in them."

"Yes, they even count it as a great advantage that their fragility has been covered over. They go so far as to thank Prometheus for taking from them their most divine qualities."

"But there is still hope for these human beings. Let us not give up on them yet. Perhaps we can even help them to enjoy again the goodness of their fragility, and not only the fragility of their goodness."

In his folly, Prometheus thought that he had stolen the fire of creativity when he had merely stolen the practical arts and that fire belonging to them.

Naked and shoeless, with neither bed nor arms of defense. Thus, open and able to share in the sharing forth of all-that-is. Able to care with and for one another and for all-that-is. Able to meet with one another, dwell with one another, and perhaps even love with one another. Yes, naked and shoeless, with neither bed nor arms of defense. Perfect. Lacking nothing. Standing in wonder before the mystery of all-that-is. Standing in awe before the mystery of others.

◆ ◆ ◆

Prometheus, who understood little of sharing, at one time warned Epimetheus never to accept a gift from the gods. But Epimetheus, knowing little of time and gifts and gods, continued to share in the sharing forth of all-that-is. With Pandora, he cared for the earth, and there was little opportunity to be concerned with time, with gifts, with gods. Enfolding one another in their hearts, Epimetheus and Pandora went along their way.

Earlier, long before all this had been forgotten, plowed under and covered over, it was said that at one time there had been no gods, and that only mortal creatures existed. It was then that Epimetheus came to know Pandora, daughter of the all-sharing Earth. For among all that the all-sharing Earth shared forth was that care, that tending-between and tending-toward, within which and from out of which Epimetheus and Pandora came to walk upon the earth and share in the commemoration of life and death; that care from out of which and within which a world was brought forth between them.

Epimetheus and Pandora nurtured that care shared out between them. Tending to the sharing forth of all-that-is, they cherished the earth. Wherever their feet stepped, their shoulders leaned, their hands touched, life sprang forth anew. Their devotion to the Earth was without parallel.

All were amazed at the devotion of Epimetheus and Pandora, and many were eager to follow in their ways. With them, Pandora and Epimetheus shared, "We have learned of a care that goes beyond mere concern. When we first began to care for the Earth, what we saw was nothing but air and water and fire and soil. After some time, we no longer saw air and water and fire and soil. Today, we commemorate the Earth with heart-and-mind rather than merely look at it with our eyes. Our sense organs stop interfering, and we move throughout as it pleases. In accord with the ways of sharing, we unfold the vital energies of incipient tendency and immanent renewal. Following the ways of the Earth, we never encounter the slightest obstacle even where the mountains and oceans come together or where humans and gods join up. A good care-giver brings forth new life now and then because she holds herself in reserve. And an ordinary care-giver unfolds new life now and then because he discriminates. Now we have been caring for the Earth without reserve, without discrimination and have helped to share out myriad things. Between all things there are empty spaces, but caring stretches between all spaces. Because we are stretching between empty spaces, we encounter no problem in caring for all."

◆ ◆ ◆

Exposed and entrusted to one another, exposed and entrusted to the Earth, Pandora and Epimetheus were brought into that covenant of peace which was before all wars and strife. Exposed and entrusted to one another, exposed and entrusted to the Earth, they stood with one another, naked and vulnerable. Their fragility was not late in coming to them, but composed their very being, with-one-another.

◆ ◆ ◆

In caring for the earth, Epimetheus and Pandora met again and again for the first time. Cherishing that wonder between them, they shared in the mystery that surrounds and sustains. In drawing near to one another, they participated again and again in that sharing through which the mystery that surrounds and sustains might attain voice and body, appearing and being heard. Again and again they renewed the tending-between and tending-toward in which the wonder of the world might come forth. Preparing themselves to reclaim—and to be reclaimed by—the mystery that precedes the world, sharing in its silence, they drew near to one another again and again.

Again and again they nurtured the silence between them. Again and again they brought forth within them and between them an openness through which they entered. Again and again they brought forth a pause between them. And were thus able to wait. The desire and the need to fill the open, the pause with words, with actions, with conventions dropped away. Again and again, a fertile silence could enter. A silence to which they were prepared to listen—though at times it had nothing to say to them.

They did not rush to fill the silence and give it words, thereby dissipating the silence in advance of its arrival, but practiced that patience through which silence comes and speaks of its own accord. Thus they did not break the silence even when they spoke. Their speech was but the beginning of a silence without end. Their words were but an articulation of that silence which can only be shared.

A vital breath was shared between them.

Pandora and Epimetheus did not try to fill the emptiness between them. In this way, they brought forth many children—and their children were thus a fruit of their care and their love rather than the product of any lack, of any need, of any injunction. Their children, like their parents, did not try to fill the emptiness between them. And in this way, they too brought forth many children.

Between Pandora and Epimetheus there was a shared desire. With one another, from out of this shared desire they brought forth many children with many names. Among their many children were Radiance, Joy, and Blossom. They were so named for it was out of their parents' many loves that they were born.

Epimetheus and Pandora wandered over the face of the earth. And everywhere they wandered, there they dwelled. Erring now here, now there, their home was always with them. Threading the valleys, crossing the plains, climbing high mountains: their sojourning was a dwelling, their dwelling a sojourning.

Heaven was under their feet as well as over their heads.

The devotion of Epimetheus and Pandora for one another was an altar upon the earth. Each one's body was a pathway to the divine. Exerting themselves to the utmost, they extended themselves toward one another, bringing forth between them the divine. Together they celebrated marvelous festivals of joy, their laughter blessing the earth. Together they silently smiled at their ever-recurring good fortune. Together they shared their breath with one another. Together, each was to the other a rare and precious treasure. Together they brought forth between them a love that could only be shared.

Thus they sailed upon an ocean of wisdom.

They rejoiced with food in their mouths. They wandered with their bellies full. Later, scarcity was forced upon them.

◆ ◆ ◆

There stood Prometheus, anxiously waiting for daybreak.

◆ ◆ ◆

Later, the offspring of Epimetheus and Pandora came to settle down alongside a field opened and cleared. There, they tilled the soil and cultivated the vine. There, they raised up edifices. And there, they came to forget both the sharing forth of all-that-is and that caring their parents had nurtured between them. No longer tending to the ways of the Earth, the offspring of Epimetheus and Pandora gave birth to new gods. New gods for new dwellings. And these new gods in turn gave birth to others, each dwelling at an ever greater distance from those to whom they owed their existence.

Sharing: the swaying movement of all that is.

And still season follows upon season, and nothing dies forever. Again and again the earth shares forth myriad things. And light follows upon dark, the warm upon the cold, the moist upon the dry, and life follows upon death. Each shares with each, coming together and pulling apart. Each shares with each—arising together, coming together, departing together. The knot of existence so firmly tied together in and through this sharing that none stands apart from the others.

The End of Agri-Culture and the Renewal of Sharing

Let us attempt to participate in sharing—not merely to stand at a distance from sharing, making of it an object, but rather to share in sharing. Sharing is the way. This is not a solitary way. It can only be shared.

The following text, like any text, does not stand alone. It calls, albeit obliquely, upon a great number of written texts and lived experiences that will perhaps appear to be only indirectly related to it. Nevertheless, these texts and experiences provide the contour, the horizon, as well as the texture, of this text. These texts and experiences can perhaps be best indicated with the words *sharing*, *gift/giving*, and *economy*—provided, of course, that these words are not understood merely in some ordinary sense; that is, provided that each of these words is thoughtfully and thankfully attended to. What is indicated, what is at stake with economy, gift/giving, and sharing is much more than is ordinarily taken to be the case. The experiences these words serve to convey are not a subset of human experience, an ontic region studied by a science or theoretical discourse. Rather, what is indicated with economy, gift/giving, and sharing is all-that-is. These are elemental words pointing us toward deeply rooted experiences—which means that we open ourselves to a certain risk by turning our intellectual, but more importantly our existential, attention toward them.

We are asking:

1. What does it mean that agri-culture in the present age has entered its final stage?
2. What renewal of sharing remains possible at the end of agri-culture?

1. What does it mean that agri-culture in the present age has entered its final stage?

Our culture is an agri-culture. Perhaps this is neither said nor thought about often enough. It has the weight of self-evidence—and like all self-evidence it usually goes without saying. Yet like all self-evidence, upon saying, and even more upon

13

being thought about, it dissolves, if not into absurdity, into a contingency from which it is difficult to recover.

While it is through a lens of self-evidence that we make our way through the world—and our lives would be short indeed without the support and guidance of some self-evidence—this in no way implies the necessity of any particular self-evidence, nor the neutrality or goodness of any particular self-evidence. The challenge is to see through otherwise the self-evidence of our agri-culture; to allow that which preceded, but does not merely lie behind it, to show itself otherwise—not as "it really was," but in an altogether other manner than has hitherto been the case.

Our agri-cultural existence has *plowed under and covered over* more than merely certain forms of flora and fauna. It has occluded, even as it modulates, earlier ways of our being-in-the-world. This agri-cultural life has long since become so familiar to us that we have a difficult time perceiving, and more importantly experiencing, all that precedes it, all that exceeds it, all that made and continues to make it possible. We now identify being human with being agricultural. And yet nothing would appear more ridiculous when looked at from the distance of ages. From such a perspective, perhaps we can begin to overcome the self-evidence that this agri-cultural existence now has for us. Perhaps we can begin to see that so much of who we are, of who we continue to be, was laid out in and through our interminable non–agri-cultural wanderings. Perhaps we can learn to draw upon otherwise, or to be drawn to otherwise, our inheritance from these times—through sharing, through caring, through meeting, through dwelling, through loving.

We forget the lengthy struggles that took place in order that we might become sedentary creatures. Our sedentary lives are like immense dams stopping up great meandering waters, allowing some of these waters to continue to spill through—and if some of this channeling was required to construct the world in which we now live, it was in no way necessary, despite the weight of its self-evidence.

It is not a matter of renouncing our sedentary existence, of attempting to return to a nomadic life of hunting and gathering or of pastoralism. Nothing could be more naïve. And yet, to assume that we have nothing to learn from our earlier existence is worse than naïve—it is stupid, not to mention dangerous. This earlier existence continues to exert an influence upon us—albeit in ways largely constructed to advance certain forms of sedentary existence. Our challenge is to see whether this earlier existence can be made to unfold otherwise than has been the case hitherto. Can we draw upon—or be drawn to—in new ways who we more primordially are?

Who are we? We have become agri-cultural.

Agri-culture is the cultivation of the field. Cultivation points toward a particular manner of dwelling; a manner of dwelling that preserves and cares for the soil and the vine; a manner of dwelling that raises up edifices. And field here points toward the setting aside and settling down alongside of a clearing distinct from its surroundings. Through and within this setting aside and settling down alongside, there can be a cultivation of the soil, of the vine, and a construction of edifices. And on the basis of this setting aside and settling down alongside there can be an appropriation and fixing—of boundaries, of property. This appropriation and fixing can be reinforced and secured through an investment of time, of labor, of life within the clearing of the field. This investment is itself a further appropriation and fixing. All subsequent appropriation and fixing hearken back to and presuppose this investment and the originary setting aside and settling down alongside.

Agri-culture, as the cultivation of the field, is first the opening and clearing of a reserve. That which is to be set aside, reserved, must first be opened and cleared. Through and within the reserve opened and cleared there can be that dwelling that preserves and cares for the soil and vine, that dwelling that raises up edifices. The opening and clearing of a reserve is a manner of dividing and distributing—of dividing and distributing what lies within and what lies without, a manner of dividing and distributing what lies within *from* what lies without. And in this way, agri-culture is an economy—a particular manner of dividing and distributing (a *nomos*) through which a reserve (an *oikos*) is opened and cleared; and, more importantly, a particular manner of acquiring those goods needed to sustain life.

This particular manner of acquiring the goods needed to sustain life has become the privileged way of acquiring these goods. This acquisition refers first to the opening and clearing of the reserve, the field. And then this acquisition refers to the myriad ways of tilling the soil, cultivating the vine, raising up edifices. It is not insignificant that agri-culture is ordinarily understood only in this latter sense. This limitation of its meaning is a part of that occluding of the past from which we are only now slowly emerging; a part of that occluding of the way in which the field of agri-culture is first opened, cleared, set aside; a part of that occluding of the meaning, the significance of this setting aside, this opening and clearing.

Within the field set aside, there is a setting upon—a setting upon that arranges and challenges the field to provide energy that can be extracted and stored. The field opened and cleared is set upon, arranged, challenged, and ordered to provide energy that can be dug up, pulled out, and stored. The field is made to work. Where previously there was a sharing out of now this and now that, the field is made to yield, to give out and to give up what has been arranged for and ordered. In the growing of grain and the grain grown, in the tending of livestock and the livestock tended, the field opened and cleared is set upon, arranged, and challenged to provide an energy that can be unlocked, taken up, appropriated, accumulated, stocked up.

It has been said that only with the advent of the modern mechanized food industry and everything it represents is there this challenging that unlocks, exposes, transforms, stores up, and distributes; that the peasant working in the field sets the field in order without setting upon the field, that the peasant's work does not challenge the soil of the field but instead cares for and maintains it. Yet in both cases, the field is challenged to provide energy that can be extracted and stored. In both cases, the setting-in-order of the field is a setting upon that strives to more efficiently unlock and expose all the field holds. In both cases, what nature holds is set upon as concealed. What is concealed is to be unlocked. Having been unlocked, it can be transformed. Transformed, it can be stored up. Stored up, it can then be used and distributed in various ways. If there is a difference between the peasant's working of the field and the mechanized food industry, it is largely a difference in intensity and efficiency.

The field being set upon and challenged to provide energy that can be extracted and stored as such does not await the modern mechanized food industry. The possibilities of the mechanized food industry are prepared for in advance in the simple growing of grain and tending of livestock. And although this simple cultivation of the field does not lead inevitably and straightaway to such modern possibilities, their way is prepared well in advance of their arrival. And if what is challenged forth through this simple cultivation is not yet the standing-reserve of contemporary technology, the way to this standing-reserve is prepared for in advance, and a place is made for it within the opening and clearing of the field. The peasant's working of the field and that of the modern mechanized food industry are infinitely closer to one another, despite all their differences, than either one is to what preceded the advent of agri-culture.

Within the field set aside and set upon, there is a push for an ever higher yield at an ever lower expense. In the simple growing of grain and the tending of livestock, a way is prepared for the contemporary demand for a maximum yield at a minimum expense. In the simple growing of grain and tending of livestock, indeed, even before them, there is a regulating and securing through which the way to this higher yield at lower expense is pursued. This regulating and securing begin with and through the opening and clearing of the field. They are extended, accelerated, and intensified in that setting upon the field through which the field is arranged and ordered—an extension, acceleration, and intensification that serve to protect and preserve what has been set aside, set upon, challenged forth, and laid up. Thus, regulating and securing do not merely characterize contemporary technology but are a characteristic of agri-culture from and with its beginnings. The regulating and securing of contemporary technology are but the latest avatars, ever more thorough and efficient, of a long process.

Who accomplishes all of this? Obviously, human beings. But human beings are brought forth through and within agri-culture as well as being the ones who bring agri-culture forth. Through and within the opening and clearing of the field, we too are set aside, set upon, and challenged. Setting aside, setting upon, challenging: these are not merely activities done by human beings. Insofar as we do not stand outside this setting aside and setting upon, we too are domesticated. Indeed, our domestication precedes and prepares the way for the domestication of crops and livestock. And we have scarcely begun to contemplate the significance of this, our own, domestication.

With this domestication, our dwelling—our stay upon the earth, a stay that is first and foremost an erring, a wandering—is fundamentally changed. We come to set aside and set upon the field. Ours becomes a life that breathes its own breath again and again. Our comings and goings are henceforth guided by that hearth-side from which we set out in the morning and to which we return each night. This domestication of our ethos—that is, of our habits, our characters, our dwelling-places, our ethics—is a domestication of our dwelling.

If the fundamental character of dwelling is to spare and preserve, it is not clear that this sparing and preserving is best articulated in and through the tilling of soil, the cultivating of the vine, the shepherding of the flock, the raising up of edifices. For we dwell upon this earth long before becoming shepherds, long before settling down within agri-culture—and our dwelling is in no way exhausted in such possibilities. Nor is it exhausted in agri-culture coming to an end.

What is meant by the end of agri-culture? Certainly not its cessation, its termination, its disappearance, its replacement by something else. Rather, the end of agri-culture is its development and completion in and into modern industrial agri-business.

It may appear as though we have entered a new age with the advent of industrialization and its recent development of information technologies. And with the exploration and commercialization of space, are we not leaving the earth, and with it agri-culture, behind? No great vision is needed to see that the agri-culture now entering its final stage has all along been determined and guided by a Promethean desire to no longer be dependent upon the earth. Modern industrialization and contemporary information technologies still set upon, arrange, and order within the field opened and cleared through and within the beginning of agri-culture. That they remain silent with regard to this does not change their dependence upon the opening and clearing of the field on which they are grounded and within which they unfold. They are modes of agri-culture, and are only thinkable within its closure. In no way do they fundamentally challenge or transform agri-culture.

From its various beginnings, a decisive aspect of agri-culture appears: the tendency to appropriate what lies beyond its horizon; to extend the opening and clearing of the field so that nothing remains outside or beyond its reserve; to bring everything to stand within the reserve opened and cleared. Along with this extension of the opening and clearing of the field comes another equally decisive aspect: the tendency to ever more thoroughly and efficiently exploit all that lies within the opening and clearing of the field; to progressively bring all that lies within the field under an arrangement and ordering that allows for its being disposed.

In the development of agri-culture in and into modern industrial agri-business, we see simultaneously its becoming worldwide and its ever more thorough and efficient setting upon, arranging, and ordering of all within the field opened and cleared. Agri-culture no longer has, and for some time has not had, an outside. It has gathered the entirety of the earth within its opening and clearing. It has become worldwide. The end of agri-culture proves to be that ever more thorough and efficient setting aside and setting upon through which everything comes to stand as standing-reserve within the field opened and cleared.

The development of agri-culture in and into modern industrial agri-business is a legitimate completion of agri-culture. Agri-culture is ending in the present age. This end proves to be the ever more thorough and efficient setting upon, arranging, and ordering of the world, of all that lies within the field opened and cleared, that takes place in and through industrialization and its contemporary applications of information technologies.

But is the end of agri-culture in the sense of its development into modern industrial agri-business also the complete realization of all the possibilities within the opened and cleared field of agri-culture? *And, more importantly, is agri-culture the sole criterion of our world sojourn?* Is the end of agri-culture in the sense of its development in and into modern industrial agri-business a complete realization of all the possibilities of that which preceded and prepared for the opening and clearing of the field? Or are there other possibilities apart from the last possibility that we characterized (the unfolding of agri-culture in and into modern industrial agri-business), possibilities from which a new understanding and experience of that which precedes and exceeds agri-culture would have to start out, but which within and as agri-culture it could perhaps not experience and adopt, or only do so with great difficulty?

Are there other possibilities still reserved for that which preceded and prepared for agri-culture that agri-culture will have concealed from its various beginnings and up to its end, other possibilities accessible neither to simple agriculture nor to modern industrial agri-business? Therefore we ask:

2. What renewal of sharing remains possible at the end of agri-culture?
Sharing and agri-culture—what does the one have to do with the other? Why and how is sharing to be renewed at the end of agri-culture? Of what sharing is it a question of renewal? We will attempt to respond to these questions in such a way that we share in the opening up of a way toward the sharing to be renewed. This response will in no way exhaustively answer these questions—particularly if this means doing away with them as questions.

The sharing to be renewed is a sharing that precedes and prepares for agri-culture. This is a sharing that sustains agri-culture in and through all of its various manifestations—and that does so without in any way being exhausted by agri-culture. Preceding and preparing for agri-culture as well as sustaining it, the sharing with which we are here concerned is thus not a more perfect distribution of what has been set upon, arranged, ordered, and appropriated within the field opened and cleared. Despite whatever need there is for such a distribution and despite whatever benefits such a distribution would yield, the sharing to be renewed is not merely another possibility within agri-culture but rather a sharing that grounds and sustains agri-culture—even when agri-culture tends to plow under and cover over this sharing.

Within the field opened and cleared, sharing is taken to come after a reserve has been generated and gathered from that which has been set aside and set upon. Within the field of this agri-cultural economy, sharing would be the distribution of a reserve. Without the reserve generated and gathered through setting aside and setting upon, sharing would be without resource. Without this reserve, where would sharing make its start, from where would it draw its funds? Must there not be a reserve to be shared? Beyond what has been set aside and set upon, where can that which is to be shared be found? Beyond what has been set aside and set upon, how could there be any sharing?

Thus, within the field opened and cleared, sharing is taken to be constrained by economy and the promises of economy. Absent some economy (and not just any economy, but a "good" economy, a productive economy) through which absence would be eliminated and a reserve accumulated, sharing would be without resource. On this account, sharing would be a dependent offspring finding its resource in some fortunate progenitor.

And yet, must sharing await all this? Must sharing presuppose this prior generation and gathering? Or is there a sharing that precedes any setting aside and setting upon as well as the reserve generated and gathered therein? Is there a sharing that remains even in and through the restrictions, limitations, and occlusions of agri-culture? Is there a sharing through which agri-culture, in all its forms, is sustained and supported; a sharing that agri-culture would take up and without which it would be without resource? If so, the renewal of this sharing would not be a matter of throwing off agri-culture in order to be done with it. There would remain even within agri-culture, indeed even within the occlusions of agri-culture, the possibility to renew this sharing.

To ask then what renewal of sharing remains possible at the end of agri-culture would not be to engage in nostalgia or a shallow romanticism. The renewal sought would not be a return to or reenactment of some event or way of life taking place in the past. Yet nor would this renewal be accomplished in some future. For such sharing is not exhausted in any present or making present. With the renewal of sharing, time and temporality are renewed. Past, present, and future are again approached and experienced as possibilities.

To ask what renewal of sharing remains possible at the end of agri-culture is to ask how we can share in that sharing forth that precedes and prepares for agri-culture; how we can share in that sharing forth that does not merely sit in the past but that sustains agri-culture throughout its various manifestations. This is a sharing that does not await a setting aside and a setting upon; a sharing that does not await the gathering of any appropriation or accumulation; a sharing that precedes any overcoming of scarcity; a sharing not reducible to nor exhausted in the distribution and partition of what has been gathered; a sharing that shares in the sharing-forth of all-that-is.

Where is such a sharing to be found? Is there a way toward such a sharing, and if so, how might we find our way toward it? And in finding our way, draw near to this sharing and share in it?

Such sharing is all around us. Even through and within agri-culture, this sharing remains with us, supporting and sustaining all that we do. But here and there, this sharing is articulated in ways that can astonish and astound. Here and there, this sharing is articulated through caring, through meeting, through dwelling, and through loving. But if we are to approach this sharing by way of caring, meeting, dwelling, and loving, we must be patient. For the way will be long. Our ways of sharing have become, in important respects, agri-cultural. And as such, they too can occlude a sharing that is other than agri-cultural as well as the ways toward such sharing. But insofar as caring, meeting, dwelling, and loving precede agri-culture and help to prepare the ground for it, they carry within them multiple paths to the sharing in question. We cared for and with one another, met with one another, dwelled with one another, and loved with one another long before settling down alongside the opened and cleared field of agri-culture. And a renewal of these ways of being with one another can put us on the path toward that sharing to be renewed at the end of agri-culture.

Wherever there is caring, or meeting, or dwelling, or loving, there sharing already prevails. Only through this sharing do our various ways of being-with-one-another come into the world. And even though our ways of caring, of meeting, of dwelling, of loving have long tended toward being reduced to forms of giving and receiving, to forms of giving and taking, if not to mere forms of exchange, they nevertheless rest upon a certain sharing. This sharing is articulated in all our ways of being-with-one-another. And it is this sharing that is taken up and taken over within agri-culture and then expressed in the various forms of giving, receiving, and exchange to which our relations with one another are thereby subjected.

Within the field opened and cleared, there is a movement or transfer *from* one *to* another. This movement or transfer can take various forms, ranging from economic exchange to the giving of gifts. Whatever form such movement takes, it implies a space and time, a spacing and temporalization in which everything is laid out, arranged, and determined in advance—a spacing and temporalization that require the building of bridges from one to another who are taken to be held or to stand apart. Yet whatever movement there is *from* one *to* another *takes* place—and this taking is to be understood in several senses—and can only take place within the *with* of a sharing. For we are with one another before any thing passes from one to another. That is, we share with one another before any one gives to or exchanges with another.

Long before settling down alongside the field opened and cleared, we are exposed and entrusted to one another, and we are exposed and entrusted to the earth. To be exposed and entrusted is to be held through and within caring. This caring is an opening and a clearing that precede the opening and clearing of the field (and the modes of cooperation that agri-culture entails). The opening and clearing of caring is an opening and clearing between us, between us and all that surrounds us.

It is in and through caring that we are first brought together, bringing us to belong with and to one another. *We are not first there and then come to be with one another. It is in being with one another that we are there at all, that there is a there, a world in which we can live and love, thank and think.* It is in and through caring that a world is opened not only in which we can live but within which all-that-is can find a place into which it is admitted. It is caring that draws us into the world. It is caring that sends us along our way. And it is through and within caring that we enjoy our stay upon the earth, our sojourn here.

To care is to attend—that is, to tend between and to tend toward. In the tending-between of caring there is place and occasion for the giving and receiving of care. But before any giving and receiving, caring shares in a sharing that is not accomplished once and for all, that is not accomplished at all. Rather, caring opens, caring shares-forth a place and occasion for all-that-is, a place and occasion into which all-that-is might be admitted.

Such caring is not a feeling or disposition of one for another. Nor is it an activity or product of us. It is not given as a gift, nor is it traded or exchanged in the manner of some possession. It does not belong to any one. Rather, caring is shared between. We share in this caring—and by way of caring we are first brought forth and brought together, brought forth in being brought together. We are a consequence of caring. As such, we do not care just now and then; rather, we are at all only through and within such caring. And within the stretching-between and stretching-toward of caring, we can share in sharing in (a) new way(s)—that is: through meeting, dwelling, loving.

It is through and within caring that we meet with one another. To meet with one another is to attend to and to tend for that openness which opens up in a mutual stretching-toward. In meeting, we draw near to one another, and in drawing near we share in bringing forth the mystery within us and between us, share in letting that mystery appear (as mystery), share in letting that mystery be heard and given voice.

The caring through which we are brought forth into this world can take place without our meeting, without our drawing near to the mystery of one (for) another. We can be with one another without meeting with one another—and, sadly, much of our being with one another, particularly within the confines of agri-culture, is impoverished in this way. Still, upon meeting, our caring for one another can be shared in more accomplished ways. In meeting, we span the dimension that stretches between us, we draw near to one another, and in drawing near we tend for the between and reverence the toward. That is to say, in drawing near to one another we draw one another further into caring.

This drawing near is not a relation of physical proximity—no exertion of the legs can bring it about. Indeed, contact is no guarantee of having met. All too often, we touch without ever meeting with one another. Within the confines of agri-culture, we are all too often alongside one another in a forced and hurried manner, coming and going from one another without attending to our being together. Rather than being a time of celebration, a time to thoughtfully attend to those with whom and for whom we care, our being with one another is too often submitted to the demands of a world poor in care, a world poor in thought; a thankless and thoughtless world. And if responding to the demands of such a world is a part of our caring with and for each other, it is neither the alpha nor the omega of this care.

Within the tending-between and tending-toward of caring, we are with others. There are, however, myriad ways of being with others. To be with others as other to each other, as openings onto the mystery that surrounds—an opening and mystery we can only enjoy in sharing it with others—is to meet with others. To be with others in ways other than this is to take or receive the other as less than other—a "less than" that results from the other being taken or received in terms of some positive or definitive concern. Whatever the concern of this taking or receiving, it falls short of that caring which can only be shared.

Meeting is a caring that can only be shared. One cannot be made to meet with another. No force is sufficient to bring it about. And if in our meeting there is giving and receiving, or giving and taking, or mere exchange, this rests upon a sharing. A meeting is not a possession or property to give to or receive from another. It is not something that can be exchanged from one to another. Rather, we meet *with* one another.

It is also through and within caring that we dwell with one another, and in dwelling meet with one another again and again for the first time. To dwell is not first or foremost to persist through spaces by virtue of our stay among things and locations. Nor is it to settle down alongside the field opened and cleared. It does not even presuppose a forest clearing in contrast to dense forest. Our stay among things and locations is preceded by and rooted in that caring through and within which we are brought forth in being brought together, that caring that sends us along our way with and to others. Through and within this caring, we span the dimension that stretches between us. This is our first dwelling. With this caring it is not things that lie near to us. For in this caring-dwelling nothing, no-thing has come to stand between those who dwell together. Before any thing comes to stand between, there is the stretching between of caring in which at least two draw near to one another.

Caring can be said to bear dwelling in such a way that dwelling rests on caring. Caring first allows dwelling to be dwelling. Caring is what really lets us dwell. We do not attain to a dwelling place through building—be it even the building of poetic creation. All building—whether it be cultivating what produces growth out of itself, erecting things that cannot come into being and subsist by growing, or poetic creation—already rests upon caring, upon the ground opened up in a tending-between and a tending-toward. For there is nowhere to build without the place and occasion opened in the stretching between and stretching toward of caring. Nor is there any building that does not rest upon a sharing of air, of breath, of blood and the caring that brings us forth into the world. We attain to dwelling through caring. And caring, which lets us dwell, is a kind of sharing.

On the ground of this caring and sharing, we can cultivate what produces growth out of itself and erect things that cannot come into being and subsist by growing. But such building is already a consequence of the nature of dwelling. It is not its ground, let alone its grounding. This grounding takes place otherwise— in sharing and caring. For the installations of building as erecting and the taking root of building as cultivating, presuppose a prior subsistence in and on air and fluids, an immersion in the elemental. Such building presupposes a sharing of life, of breath, of blood that have been taken up and taken over. And it implies an appropriation of nature, a breaking-in and clearing of the earth—rather complex, if not accomplished, relations that presuppose a life and growth premised on a sharing of nature.

The essential nature of dwelling is manifest in the home. The home can only be shared. A house, a shelter—such things can be bought and sold, given and received. But a home can only be shared. Unlike the house, the function of which is to cover and conceal—and thereby protect us from what and who lies beyond its walls—the home serves as a privileged place and occasion for uncovering and revealing ourselves to one another while retaining our mystery. Although a house may serve to secure and guarantee our physical existence, and to do so may require a solidity closed upon itself, the home, as a place and occasion for our relations with others, is unavoidably fragile. Within the home, each remains, and must remain open to a becoming of the other or others, a becoming that is neither merely passive nor merely active. This fragility of the home and of relations with others is manifest not only in the births and deaths that take place within the home, simultaneously threatening its existence and offering to strengthen its bonds, but in all our relations with others, from the most distant to the most intimate. In all such relations we lay (ourselves) open before and to others. It is this laying (oneself) open that is put at risk in the attempt to reduce the home to a house through regulating and controlling the movements and actions of everyone within, around, and outside the home.

[A risky proposition: the origin of domestic abuse can be said to lie in this abusive reduction of home to house, to lie in the abusive reduction of our dwelling with one another to relations of force and distance.]

In the home, we do not simply live in physical proximity to one another. A home does not come about from our being placed side by side. In the home, the interval between us is to be maintained—indeed, it is to be deepened and made more fecund. Sharing this interval, we approach one another, becoming aware of the wealth of differences in our ways of being in the world and then creating ways of drawing near between us; ways of drawing near for which we may still lack words; ways of drawing near that are reducible to neither a natural unfolding nor a technical producing; ways of drawing near that, without reducing our differences in a unified identity, allow us to share places and occasions, to bring forth together the new and the unexpected, to speak with one another. What is brought forth and shared in this way—a non-divisible whole that extends between—cannot be appropriated or mastered by any one without ceasing to be.

Another name for dwelling—that is, for the sharing of the interval between us in which we lay (ourselves) open with and to others—is love. This is a love rooted within sharing and caring; a love that blossoms and bears fruit through meeting and dwelling. Like the home, this love is neither given as a gift nor is it exchanged. It is a love that can only be shared. And what is received in such love is not simply given. For only through sharing in this love can this love be received. Such love grows out of the caring and sharing through which we dwell; grows out of the relation with the other as other. And through such love we come to dwell in the world anew. This is a love between us—that is, distance in proximity—a sharing between us of that nearness which does not efface all that separates us while drawing us together.

Such love is a radicalization and intensification of dwelling. A mutually beneficial straining to respect and to nurture the singularity of each other; a mutual embracing of the finitude of each and all who hold themselves within and are held within the relation, this love seeks to bring about the growth of each one as well as of the relation between each and all. In this growth, there is an uplifting of each and all through a harmonious blending of singularities in which each enhances the other(s) and in which each retains his or her integrity.

To be on the way to such love implies a new experience and understanding of dwelling, of being-at-home in which to dwell is to err, to wander. We are at home in wandering. Wandering, we are nevertheless at home. Although this may strike us as improbable, it is not without promise. For it indicates that the openness of wandering is not foreign or antithetical to the home and being at home. And it reminds us that to foreclose wandering, to remain within a secured enclosure is to foreclose the possibility of the home and the openness it presupposes. It could thus be said that the current lovelessness of our world is not unrelated to a certain homelessness—a homelessness brought about by the domestication of our wandering, a homelessness brought about by our confinement within the field of agri-culture.

Long before the cultivation of the field—with all that this implies—there is a sharing forth of all that is, a sharing out in which all share. It is through and upon this sharing that agri-culture makes its start. And it is through this sharing that all our ways of being with one another are brought forth. With a renewal of our being with one another—a renewal of caring, meeting, dwelling, loving—we are put along the way toward a sharing that precedes and sustains agri-culture as well as those forms of exchange, of giving and receiving, of giving and taking to which our relations are subjected through and within agri-culture. With a renewal of these more primordial ways of being with one another, we can participate in bringing forth anew a sharing between us. And thus we can come to participate in that resurgence of sharing that would be a relinquishing of those forms of appropriation and mastery made possible through agri-culture, and thereby participate in a renewal of our being, together.

Sharing

> . . . sharing all with all. In this way the abundance of the earth grew, bringing forth again and again that circle of birth and death through which all were provided with a share of elemental abundance.

> . . . sharing all with all, the overflowing abundance of the earth was in no way diminished. Indeed, through such sharing abundance was shared forth again and again.

A Cosmic Sharing

This cosmos: without reserve. Its law at each moment: expenditure without return. Yet no prodigal son—perhaps rather an all-sharing mother who holds nothing back, who in sharing shares forth all that is.

This cosmos: a sharing that increases through expenditure; a sharing that does not divide, but rather multiplies; a sharing without loss, without appropriation; a sharing that in expending without return shares forth abundance again and again; a sharing beyond profit and loss.

This cosmos: yielding every place with, in, and through sharing; a sharing that is not that out of which this cosmos emerges, but the way of the cosmos; a sharing that is thus neither secondary nor derivative; a sharing that unfolds prior to any fold(ing).

This cosmos: constantly renewing itself through sharing, by way of sharing.

This cosmos: the com-posing of things; a com-posing that can only be shared (and in being shared is com-posed); an arranging in which all things share; an order that is not imposed from on high, from some transcendent beyond—but that emerges spontaneously again and again from the com-position of things; whose com-position spontaneously engenders order; whose com-position is the propensity, the tendency of things.

This cosmos: a com-posing without a composer.

This cosmos: neither created nor fashioned, yet always emerging such as it is.

This cosmos: thus not an order in which things are dis-posed; not the space or scene or (temporal) unfolding of an antagonism or agonistics; not a scene of confrontation.

This cosmos: a marvelous wonder—not only *that* it is, but *how* it is.

This cosmos: now systole, now diastole; intensification, dilation, transformation.

This cosmos: a great dragon; with no fixed form, no definitive shape; now unfolding, now coiling up again; impossible to grasp once and for all.

This cosmos: a great conflagration without beginning or end; ever raging, ever renewing; an iridescence growing ever more expansive without fading; expending itself without reserve at each moment, and in doing so emerging anew again and again; at the same time both one and many; forever shifting, forever variable; increasing here while decreasing there—yet always multiplying without end as a whole; both creating and destroying—creating in destroying, destroying in creating, transforming without end. A great fire passing through all-that-is; now thunder and lightning, now dragon's breath; now great star, now humble hearth. The same great fire warming all throughout.

This cosmos: a great clod; eccentric, insubstantial. A great clod upon which, through which, out of which all-that-is emerges, unfolds, and departs; each sharing, each with its share. A great clod, now desert, now swamp; now mountain, now valley; now field, now forest. A great clod, never barren, never wasteland, never inhospitable. A great clod, yielding every place without loss, without want.

This cosmos: a great ocean without beginning or end; a fluid and fertile sharing, with vital energies of immanent renewal and incipient tendency flowing together and rushing apart; a swaying movement that grows ever more expansive without becoming diluted; a deep pool that never dries; that expends itself without reserve at each moment, and in doing so emerges anew again and again; as a whole, like a home that forever expends without reserve, yet without loss, that forever increases, yet without income; a home that while not endlessly extended is boundless; a great sea that is not empty here or there, but full with wave upon wave, fold upon fold; at the same time both one and many; forever changing, forever flooding back; increasing here while decreasing there—yet always multiplying without end as a whole; with neither creation nor destruction, but transformations without end; now this, now that; a great becoming without rest; without goal, unless the joy of sharing without reserve, ever and again, is a goal; this, our Gaia, forever sharing and sharing forth all that is; this cosmos of mystery—simultaneously this cosmos shared out in mystery and the mystery shared (through)out in this cosmos.

[Yes, everything passes. At every moment we do indeed see myriad beings destroyed as myriad beings are brought forth into existence. And each exists side by side with the others, none having any greater right to existence than the others. But it is only by taking a particular view of all this that we see nature as force devouring force. Taking this more partial perspective—this more limited and biased perspective—on the movement of existence, we may indeed see being devouring being in a war of all against all. But this interpretation has nothing necessary in it—and much that should make us suspicious of its doing justice to existence. A more vast perspective reveals the sharing flow of existence—in which there is no addition or subtraction, only multiplication and division. The movement of this sharing flow is not so much force devouring force as it is wave following upon wave—each having its moment, rising, cresting, passing away, and in this way sharing all with all.]

This cosmos: a great breath shared between us; circulating throughout; rarefied here, condensed there; not simply one, yet not a multiple of one; the same great breath shared between us, yet never identical, self-same, static; a breath that is renewed and renews itself in being shared; a breath carrying silence and song, whispers and words, cries and cacophonies; a great breath passing through all-that-is, from star to star, from life to death to life; that grows ever more expansive without becoming exhausted; this miracle of change taking place at every moment.

Elemental Sharing

There is no element, only an elemental sharing. A sharing in which each "element" is com-posed. That is, each "element" is posed with and through (all the) others, each "element" stands with and through (all the) others. Each "element" is what it is with and through (all the) others, each "element" sharing (in ex-istence) with and through (all the) others.

To stand is unavoidably to stand-with. No thing stands alone. No thing stands apart. Each stands-with (all the) others.

There can be no solitary position—be it that of some god. For every position is a com-position; every position the com-position of singular relations to other positions; every position a position with and between other positions; every position com-posed with, by, through other positions.

It is not a matter of there being elements—each with its share of being—distributed in space and time in such a way that these elements can then be brought into relation, one relation being that of sharing. Each element must already share (with and through) in order to share in existence.

The dis-position of one by or toward another; the ex-position of one to another; the juxta-position of one and another; all presuppose that elemental sharing in which each is com-posed with and through (all the) others.

This elemental sharing is not reducible to a complementarity that would unite the complements in a oneness, a whole, a totality. There is complementarity only within the com-position of things.

There are no elements, only elemental configurations. We must learn again how to count—three precedes two and one; plurality pre-cedes individuation. In plurality, there is a place for individuation; a place that is always com-posed. The "individual," far from being indivisible, an atom, is com-posed. The singularity of any "individual"—its being *this* individual and no other—lies in its com-position. In "its" com-position, each "individual" constitutes a unique, that is, singular, hinge around which all-that-is (un)folds.

[Perhaps if we were to recognize and cultivate—that is, respect and venerate—the priority of relations, we would be able to better appreciate singularity, our singularity as well as that of all that ex-ists. While this may strike as odd those who have grown up within a tradition that has *given* priority to individual entities (*ens individuum*), singularity only emerges in and through relation.

Despite a long tradition that would always begin by attempting to bring together, to conjugate, to join, to link that which it believed to be—in its origin and in itself—disparate and discrete, the challenge is to explain how singular elements or entities come to emerge from their com-positional configurations, and can emerge in such a way that the com-positional movement through which elements or entities are com-posed is lost or forgotten in favor of a substantial self-subsistence.

There are, however, other traditions—traditions that would always begin with these com-positional configurations, seeing in them the spontaneous tendency to engender order. The tendency of things—the propensity for "Z" to emerge from "X" and "Y"—emerges from the com-positional configurations of all-that-is.]

There are no elements, only elemental processes. Each sharing-with and sharing-through (all the) others: the swaying movement of all-that-is. "With" and "through" do not indicate a fullness, a plenitude—yet nor do they indicate any lack or deficiency. Rather, "with" and "through" indicate the flowing of each with and through each.

Each is an ongoing process with and through (all the) others.

Each sharing with and through (all the) others, it is not only or merely a matter of some interval separating each from each—an interval that would separate each element from what it is in order for the element to be itself, an interval that would thereby divide the element in and of itself, and so divide, along with the element, everything that is thought on the basis of the element. The sharing-with and sharing-through of each element is otherwise than—or, at least, not reducible to—this process of division and separation. To focus exclusively or too narrowly upon this process of division and separation would be to privilege the sharing-through with which each is com-posed—at the expense of that equiprimordial sharing-with through which each is com-posed. Insofar as each is com-posed with all, each sharing-with and sharing-through all, each is not only separate from, divided from (itself as well as) others. Each is with (all the) others—in an irreducibly singular way.

It is not a matter of adding to a separation and division such that each element, in addition to being divided in itself as well as from others, would also be with others. Each is always already with (all the) others.

To be com-posed with and through (all the) others is neither to be related in an allergic or antagonistic way to the others nor to be endlessly deferred by others.

There is no absolute alterity. [No other is altogether other—which in no way diminishes the mystery of any one.] Nor is there any absolute identity. Sharing-with and sharing-through, all-that-is is neither fused together in some oneness, some unity, some totality, nor is it diffused in some absolute difference or endless deferral.

[A focus on separation and division, on difference and deferral, can result as a consequence of an overemphasis on identity and presence. Rightly seeing the "constructed," "constituted" nature of the present and everything made possible through or upon it, such a thinking might easily restrict its focus on that sharing-through by which everything is com-posed. Yet perhaps there is in such a focus a tendency to overlook or neglect that sharing-with by which everything is equi-primordially com-posed. That everything is com-posed in a sharing-through does indeed entail that no thing ever settles into a stable, self-sufficient, self-presence; does indeed entail that presence-to-self or identity is an "effect" (albeit without a cause) of difference and deferral. But whereas sharing-through can be understood in terms of such difference and deferral, the same cannot be said of sharing-with. In sharing-with, it is precisely the contact, the relation, the being-posed-together *that difference and deferral presuppose* that emerges and unfolds. In sharing-with, each is posed with all the others; each is in relation with (all the) others. Thus, each is not merely an "effect" of differing and deferring, but is posed with all the others in an utterly unique, singular, non-repeatable way.]

Sharing-with and sharing-through all the others, each "element" can be said to come-to-be, tarry awhile, and depart. Each "has its share" in the swaying movement of all that is.

Each would not be what it is if it were to be otherwise.

There are no elements, only elemental relations. Each "element" is com-posed—that is, posed with—(all the) others. Thus, rather than being self-sufficient, indivisible atoms, each is a non-finite nexus of relations to other elements. Things do not first exist, and then later become dynamic and enter into relations such as that of sharing. Rather, things always con-sist. That is, they are with others, they stand together with others.

No element is ever present in and of itself, such that it would refer only to itself. Rather, every element con-sists—that is, each stands with and through (all the) others, each is com-posed with and through (all the) others. Each relates elementally with and through (all the) others.

[In thinking about and experiencing this elemental sharing, it is important to avoid thinking that first things must exist and then later become dynamic and enter into relationships such as that of sharing. If all that is "shares in existence" rather than having any independent self-existence, there is neither creation nor destruction but rather an arising and ceasing, a crest and trough, transformation upon transformation.

There are no things—perhaps only relations.

The successful emergence of each thing within experience is achieved (only) through a sharing with its environing others that entails both helping to bring forth and yielding, both making be and letting be.]

Poietic Sharing

This cosmos: neither created nor fashioned, yet always emerging such as it is.

The sharing *forth* of all-that-is: the com-posing, the standing-with of each with (all the) others. In and through the sharing *forth* of all-that-is, all things are com-posed. Each is posed-with, each stands-with (all the) others. Each emerges with and through (all the) others. That is, all things are shared *forth* in a sharing in and through, or with, one another.

To stand-with (all the) others: to be dis-posed with and toward (all the) others—where to be dis-posed is not yet to enter into an allergic or antagonistic relation. To be dis-posed is to be set in a particular order where each is inclined-toward (all the) others. To incline, to be inclined is to tend or stretch toward, to have a tendency.

Thus, in the com-posing of all-that-is, there is tendency, propensity. This tendency does not come to things from beyond; arriving to set things in motion, to direct them toward some end. In the com-posing of all-that-is, each is inclined-toward others, each tends-toward others. There is tending-toward, tendency in the com-posing of all-that-is.

Sharing forth: com-positional spontaneity; the self-transforming of all-that-is; the immanent dynamism of all-that-is.

Order, such as there is, lies within becoming rather than being imposed upon it from without. There might thus be said to be a regular and spontaneous fecundity in the com-position of things. In the very com-position of things, in the standing-with of each with all, there is an ordering of each with each, of each with all.

In the very com-position of things, there is a mingling and blending of singularities in such a way that each mutually benefits and enhances the other(s) without losing their singularity even while com-posing a frictionless whole. Thus, there is a harmony in the very com-position of things—an order that emerges out of the com-position of things, out of the alliance of singularities inhering in one another, intrinsically related to one another.

Every com-posing is a com-position, every com-position a com-posing.

There is nothing over, other than, or beyond the com-posing of all-that-is. There can be no position, or the taking of a position, over, other than, or beyond the com-position of all that is. Every position is a com-position. Every com-position a position-with. There is no before, after, outside, or beyond from which a position other than a com-position might be posed.

The com-posing of all-that-is is all that is.

The sharing forth of all-that-is: diachrony without synchrony—but not without a certain synchronization.

Sharing: the swaying breach of the ever-emerging present.

In the com-posing of things, there is a materialization without matter—insofar as matter implies a settling down, a stability. In the com-posing of things, there is stabilization without stability.

Each ordering of all-that-is (spontaneously) yielding (to) another in the ongoing sharing out of all-that-is. Each ordering yielding (to) the ongoing flux and flow of transformation.

Maternal Sharing: In the Elemental

Like all life, ours is a life that was shared before it was offered or given—which does not in any way diminish what was thus shared. More past than any memorable past, this sharing was neither accepted nor received. Rather, it was imposed—not as the law is imposed, from on high—but as a mystery that simultaneously envelops and opens. Neither a threat nor a persecution, this sharing was open, as well as an opening. It was without obligation. It did not ask for repayment. It was an open hand extended—but one that could not be refused. Thus, this sharing was the beginning of an openness toward . . . , an openness to . . . —but it was also an opening by . . . .

[Each opening by . . . presupposes a sharing-with and sharing-through without which there would be no (re)source.]

This sharing: without birth, without beginning, through which all are brought forth, born, take root, grow, and return.

This sharing of life: an inexhaustible fecundity; a bottomless productivity.

[Such fecundity, such productivity would be the groundless ground of both the installations of building as erecting and the taking root of building as cultivating. Building as erecting and building as cultivating presuppose an appropriation of nature, a breaking-in and clearing of land, a gathering and distribution of "resources"—adult, if not mature, actions premised upon a prior maternal sharing of life and growth.]

This sharing: bountiful without end—lasting and enduring because it does not live for itself; a beginning that begins at every moment; a beginning that surrounds and sustains, inspires and enthuses with energy, with spirit, with life. This sharing: with and through which all-that-is subsists; nourishing and sustaining life. Held in the hands of sharing, each is maintained in existence. Without this vital flowing, the circle of life–death in which all is held would cease to turn.

This sharing: the innocence of becoming; the ceaseless transformation of all-that-is.

This sharing: neither mine nor yours; neither his nor hers; beyond possession, a sharing between (us). Our being (-here, -in-the-world): thus, not a gift; not a giving; not that "from which" we live. Each is with and through others; with and through, sharing, each lives.

This sharing: a sharing of what is never one's to give: life; a sharing not reducible to the giving of a gift. This sharing: pre-ceding giving and the gift, ceding to them their place; sharing: the groundless ground of giving, of the gift.

Life can only be shared. It would be death and the dead that are given, exchanged—which is not to suggest that death too cannot be shared.

[There is and can be no first gift. Nor is there, nor can there be a gift without measure—and hence without debt. There was never a time when she gave herself entirely without distance or difference.]

This sharing: a mystery spontaneously giving birth.

Thus, neither she (alone) nor he (alone) gives the possibility of that beginning from which each (woman, man, world) will be com-posed. That is not one's—hers or his—to give. It can only be shared—sharing-with and sharing-through preceding that from out of which one might give. For the beginning is not a gift received—from a mother, from a father—without any possibility of return. Each beginning is born spontaneously from a sharing-with and a sharing-through; born spontaneously from a union-between; a union-between that does not arise as the result of some intentionality or cause; a sharing that does not rise to the level of consciousness or intentionality that giving and the gift imply.

This sharing: the indeterminate mother of all-that-is; a sharing in which there is no subject or object; no self or world; a sharing of each with all in which we share; each in continuity with and through all.

With and through the ongoing flow of sharing, all-that-is finds a place and occasion to come forth, to be born, to take root, to grow, and to return.

If there can be said to be any indivisible proximity, it is through sharing rather than any gift that this is possible. A sharing-with and sharing-through—in which there is simultaneously continuity and distinction. A sharing without hindering borders—his or hers. A sharing without borders, and yet without fusion.

This maternal sharing, this modest back-and-forth motion: the groundless ground of the relation-between.

Such sharing would be "lost," forgotten, denied, covered over as much when "he" uses it to produce, to fabricate a world as when "she" appropriates it as her gift. For neither is the nocturnal ground of all-that-is. Sharing: this groundless ground.

Sharing forth all-that-is; nurturing each; sharing life without managing each and all; raising each and all without lording it over them—this is called the most profound mother of all-that-is.

Wonder: An Interlude

Naked and shoeless, with neither bed nor arms of defense. Thus, open
and able to share in the sharing forth of all-that-is. Able to care with
and for one another and for all-that-is. Able to meet with one another,
dwell with one another, and perhaps even love with one another. Yes,
naked and shoeless, with neither bed nor arms of defense. Perfect.
Lacking nothing. Standing in wonder before the mystery of all-that-
is. Standing in awe before the mystery of others.

Wonder: a sharing in the sharing forth of all-that-is.

Wonder: an opening of sharing to itself; an unfolding of sharing that folds
back upon itself (and thus continues to share itself forth in this way).

Wonder: the unfathomable mystery of all-that-is.

Wonder solicits us. That is, it calls us forth, puts us in motion, moves us
throughout. It establishes and marks the entirety of who we are with solicitude.
It fills us with care.

To be solicited by wonder is not to be disturbed by some exterior force.
It is not to be overtaken or set upon by some thing or some one exterior to us;
some thing or some one that would come to disturb or disrupt a prior restfulness,
a pre-existing, and perhaps self-sufficient and self-satisfied, interiority. There is
no interiority, no there, no being-there prior to or outside of wonder. It is in and
through wonder that there is any there, any being-there. Wonder solicits being-
there—that is, it calls it forth, puts it in motion, moves it throughout.

Wonder is not some action or some thing that merely befalls us now and then. We are utterly exposed by wonder, and we are utterly exposed to wonder. We are at all only through and within wonder and our living unfolds in and upon wonder. It is not some thing we do or some thing we have. Wonder awakens us. We are an awakening of and to wonder. Indeed, we are wonder—that is, we are called forth, put in motion, moved throughout by wonder. We are not, however, the whole of wonder (assuming that there is such a thing). For aroused by wonder we share in the sharing forth of all-that-is, we share in, but do not possess—even in thought—the whole of all-that-is.

We are not overtaken by wonder as a tortoise is overtaken by a hare.

In wonder, we are overwhelmed. That is, we are moved throughout. We are not merely open to wonder. Our exposure is much more profound than that. To be open to wonder implies that we could in principle become closed. But it turns us so inside out that to close to wonder would still be to be exposed. It is through this very being turned inside out that we become who we are. We are (a being) turned inside out.

To be turned inside out is not merely to be affected by some change. It is to become who we are. It is to be brought forth, filled with solicitude. And to be filled with solicitude is not to be filled up like some more or less empty vessel. Rather, to be filled with solicitude is to be moved wholly by it. Solicitude is the motion into which we are put. This motion does not come to disturb or cause to tremble one who was previously at rest. It is the very motion of who we are—a motion of tending-toward and tending-between.

Open, without resistance. Overwhelmed in this way, we are prone to fall into wells or to stand awe-struck, silent.

That which arouses wonder can be called the mystery.

The mystery is not a nut to be cracked—but a seed to be scattered, nourished, and perhaps cultivated.

Mystery is not to be dissipated. Rather, the ground is to be prepared for its fecundation—a ground, a preparation in no way exhausted within the field of agri-culture.

A nurturing of wonder: caring, meeting, dwelling, loving . . .

A cultivation of wonder: poetry, mythology, philosophy, science, techne, history . . .

◆ ◆ ◆

There is a kind of joyful tranquility born of wonder—and it is only with the ebbing of this tranquility that any yearning for wisdom comes forth and grows. This joyful tranquility is the offspring of that opening and that openness in, through, and out of which wonder unfolds.

The wisdom of love is a wisdom of making way for and toward such tranquility—a tranquility that is not a stasis but a being placed fully and harmoniously within the swaying movement of all-that-is. The wisdom of love is a wisdom of making way for and toward a deepening of our sharing in things, a deepening of our sharing with others (through caring, through meeting, through dwelling, through loving)—a deepening, and not an allaying, of wonder.

We can make way for wonder—but wonder does not come about as a result or a product of our making. It is not within our power, our control.

◆ ◆ ◆

Wonder is no more reducible to thinking than thinking is reducible to a pursuit of knowledge or truth.

Wonder is far more primordial than thinking—and thinking, even a meditative thinking, is but one way of responding to wonder. In wonder, we are amazed, astonished. We are awe-struck.

Wonder is far more primordial than questioning—and questioning is but one way of responding to wonder. Lost in wonder, the occasion to question is still on the way.

If wonder sets us to thinking and questioning, it is not exhausted in this. For it moves us in heart-and-mind, moves us in our entirety.

If there is no response to wonder that is not a thinking or a questioning response, this is not to suggest that every response to wonder is thought-full or reducible to or exhausted in thought. And although questioning and thinking can be ways of fecundating wonder, they are not the only ways of doing so.

It has been said that a love of wisdom begins in wonder. Yet such love is not all that begins in wonder. Nor is a love of wisdom the firstborn of wonder. Wonder solicits us throughout. It moves us. It is an awakening of heart-and-mind. In this awakening of heart-and-mind there is a place and occasion for a love of wisdom. But this awakening of heart-and-mind is a place and occasion for more than mere thought. It is also a place and occasion for what has been too quickly called attunement, affect, mood, disposition. Perhaps that is why it has been said that wonder is the feeling of the lover of wisdom. For the love of wisdom unfolds within a mood, a mood solicited by wonder.

It is curious—but not wonder-full—that lovers of wisdom, despite the importance they have accorded to wonder, have failed to attend to it. Not only have they said little of wonder—and their silence in this is understandable. When they have spoken of it, they have often kept it at arm's length or wrapped it in abstractions—referring it to unmoved movers or to starry skies above or to formal laws and imperatives. Seldom have they nurtured and cultivated wonder in ways that exceed thought—for example, through caring, through meeting, through dwelling, through loving. They have too often situated themselves on the limits of wonder, confusing wonder with curiosity, confining themselves to an investigation of the curious—an investigation that has aimed, for the most part, at the dissolution or elimination of curiosity. They have too often assumed their task to be one of allaying wonder; holding wonder to obtain only insofar as reason has not yet explained some thing under consideration; assuming that by giving reasons for things being as they are they could allay wonder; acting as if an explanation of things would lead to an elimination of the occasion for wonder.

But the wonder that solicits us is not reducible to curiosity. Nor is it allayed or reduced by any investigation. Indeed, wonder need not provoke truth or knowledge, nor their pursuit or investigation.

It happens, perhaps inevitably, that wonder comes to be seen as befalling us, as coming along and in some way disturbing our everyday way of being in the world. And in a certain sense, this can be said to be the case. But we can only be overtaken or overcome with wonder in this way because wonder solicits us entirely.

◆ ◆ ◆

To be struck with wonder—this is not merely to be stopped in our tracks, nor is it to be lost or to be without a way out. For we are not struck with wonder now and then. Being struck with wonder does not simply result in not knowing where we are going or where our path may lead.

Wonder is not to be put behind us—as if with the moment of wonder having passed we can now "get down to business."

◆ ◆ ◆

Wonder is neither a faculty nor an operation of the mind or of the spirit. It is not some faculty that might atrophy if it is not sufficiently exercised—although we can become so closed to wonder that our awareness of being moved by wonder is limited to those unsurpassable moments of birth, of death. In being closed thus to wonder, we wander away from our essential nature. That is, we wander away from wonder.

Although wonder is not a faculty that would be at our disposal, there is a certain openness and opening without which wonder will not come to pass. But this opening and openness are themselves part of wonder and not merely external conditions for it.

We are disposed by wonder. And to be disposed by wonder is to be disposed to wonder.

◆ ◆ ◆

Solicited by wonder, it can appear possible to track down wonder; to retrace the steps back to wonder; to search it out. But the path to be followed is like a deer path that suddenly comes to an end without any sign of where to go.

◈ ◈ ◈

Wonder solicits us. Wonder sets us on the way of solicitude. The way of solicitude is a way of awe and anticipation.

◈ ◈ ◈

Wonder always awaits us.

Caring

Before the gods, men and women were exposed and entrusted to one another. Abiding with one another, there was neither host nor guest. Nor was one the hostage of another. No one stood above any other. They walked the earth together, hand in hand. And in this way, they shared in the commemoration of all-that-is. There was not then the giving and taking, the giving and receiving that would later come to stand between humans as well as between humans and the gods. Words had not yet been brought forth, casting rainbows and illusive bridges between things forever apart. Nor had any sacrifice been offered, casting rainbows and illusive bridges between things forever as one. Rather, each shared with each in the swaying movement of creation.

Wonder

It begins in wonder—a wonder that it begins at all.

Miraculous: the tending-between and tending-toward of caring; the awakening of hearts-and-minds.

Caring: the sharing forth of a between and a toward in which there is (the worlding of) a world.

Doubly miraculous: the tending-between and tending-toward of caring and all that appears thereby. It is a wonder that there is caring. It is a wonder that there is wonder. There is not the least reason for caring to be shared forth. It is only through and within the tending-between and tending-toward of caring that there is anywhere for wonder and the wonder-full—that is, all-that-is—to appear.

45

[One name for such wonder is Being—but it is only one such name.]

Naked and shoeless, with neither bed nor arms of defense. Thus, open and able to share in the sharing forth of all-that-is. Able to care with and for one another and for all-that-is. Able to meet with one another, dwell with one another, and perhaps even love with one another. Yes, naked and shoeless, with neither bed nor arms of defense. Standing in wonder before the mystery of all-that-is. Standing in awe before the mystery of others.

Mysterious: the ways in which we belong together and to the earth.

From Tendency to Attending

Sharing: the groundless ground of caring. Through the sharing forth of all-that-is, all that lives is com-posed—that is, each comes to stand with all the others in a singular way. Each way of standing with all the others is a tendency, a being-inclined-toward. Among the myriad tendencies is a tendency to attend. To attend is to care—that is, to tend-between and to tend-toward.

This caring, before being the action of some one toward or upon some other, is a tending-between in which one and an other can surge forth, each inclined toward the other(s). Thus, this caring is not an activity or product of us. We are a consequence of caring. We no longer mean by caring a feeling or disposition of one for another. With caring, each and all are *with* one another before there is any one-for-another. There can only be a one-*for*-another within the being-*with* of one *and* an other.

This being-with-one-another is a being-exposed with and to one another—a being-exposed in which each lays bare and is laid bare with and before others; a being-exposed that would belie any supposed self-sufficiency.

◆ ◆ ◆

The sharing forth of tending-between and tending-toward opens and clears. This opening and clearing of caring is the ex-tending of every place and occasion into which all-that-is might be admitted. For only through and within the tending-between and tending-toward is any place and occasion provided for appearing, disclosure, manifestation. All-that-is appears and unfolds through and within the between and toward of caring.

Caring is the unfolding of being-there-together. The spatiality of being-there unfolds through and within the originary orientation of tending-between and tending-toward. Being-there is thus a being-there-with, a being-there-together in and through caring.

With caring, as the unfolding of being-there-together, there is no first one on the scene. Any scene, any there, is itself the unfolding of a sharing between those who are with one another. Hence, the there of being-there is proper to no one. It is shared between.

All-that-is is shared between (us)—yielded between; never given, only shared. In caring, there is place and occasion for the giving and receiving of care. But before any giving and receiving, caring shares in a sharing that is not accomplished once and for all, that is not accomplished at all. This caring is not Promethean, but Epimethean.

[Perhaps the day will come when we will no longer shun that caring that opens and clears, no longer shun that caring within which alone space and time and all-that-is share in the place and occasion that shares them forth.]

Being-With

Our sojourn, our stay begins through caring. Caring sends us along the way, along our way. Caring draws us into this world. In and through caring, we are exposed and entrusted—with and to others, to the earth. Our being, like all being, is thus a being-with.

Our being-with is a being exposed—a being exposed with and to one another. It is a being open to one another—a being open that lays bare, sharing our fragility with one another.

◆ ◆ ◆

Through and within the sharing forth of life there can be the tending-between and tending-toward of caring, a tending in which one and an other are first brought forth and brought together, brought forth in being brought together. To be brought forth in being brought together is not to be placed side by side, face to face. It is, rather, to be exposed with and to one another.

◆ ◆ ◆

In and through caring, that innermost essence of who we are reaches outward most fully and to the outermost limits. It does this so decisively that the notion of an inner and an outer world does not arise. In and through caring, all that touches us is gathered together (gathered together as shared out between us).

Caring is not an externalization—not even an externalization without any prior internalization. It is, rather, our com-position, our ex-position.

◆ ◆ ◆

Our being-with neither begins in nor aims toward a fusion, a oneness without difference and distance. Nor is it reducible to a collectivity, a community, a solidarity—particularly one organized and oriented around a (search for) truth. It is not a side-by-side, a one-by-one. It is prior to any one-for-another, be it that of a face-to-face—indeed, it is in our being-with-one-another that we are brought face to face with one another. Our exposure in being-with-one-another is much more profound than merely being side by side or even face to face. The entirety of who we are is held within and unfolds through our being-with-one-another. It is the exposure of a newborn baby; unable to turn away; with no where to hide; utterly exposed, exposed through and through. Thus, this is not the exposure of an infancy that will be erased with time. Rather, it constitutes us through and through. And yet we lose none of our mystery through this exposure—indeed, the mystery of each one is spared, preserved, fecundated, and grows more profound in our being-with-one-another.

Our being-with articulates both a between and a toward, an unbridgeable distance in proximity and a contact without coincidence. It articulates both proximity and distance; distant because proximate, proximate because distant. Hence, there is here no (fear of) losing oneself and the other in a Same, a One, a totality. There is here no need for a supposedly non-relational relation—supposedly without intermediary, without communion; supposedly *absolute* proximity and *absolute* distance simultaneously.

◆ ◆ ◆

We do not care just now and then; rather, we are who we are at all only through and within such caring.

Caring, our essential nature, is not a gift given to us. It is shared (forth) between us. We may receive many gifts, of many kinds. But we can only receive gifts insofar as we share in the sharing forth of all-that-is in a manner befitting our being. That is, we can only receive gifts insofar as we care. Caring is not something that one can do by one's self. Indeed, caring is that through which one comes to be who one is. In this sense, one never (quite, merely, simply) gives or receives a gift, but shares in the giving of whatever is given.

Caring, the essential agreement, comes before and is the condition for that possibility of failing to agree, failing to care. Only because it is our essential nature to care can we be careless. Only because it is our essential nature to care can we fail to attend to others. That is to say, even our failure to care presupposes the tending-between and tending-toward of caring. Carelessness—a neglect and forgetting of the other; a denial of the other, of the other's singularity; separation; violence; murder; atheism—presupposes care. Our failure to care is a mode, albeit deficient or impoverished, of tending-between and tending-toward.

To have been brought into the world through care is to be denied atheism. Atheism is, at best, a kind of carelessness, a forgetting of our essential nature, a wandering away from our essential nature. Yet just as we can only be careless because it is our essential nature to care, so we can only be "godless" because it is our essential nature to share in the divine.

◆ ◆ ◆

One symptom of having wandered away from our essential nature—while never having simply lost it—is the dissociation of heart and mind. In caring, heart-and-mind belong together. There is no caring that does not carry together heart-and-mind.

◆ ◆ ◆

Caring: a covenant of peace before all wars and strife.

In caring, there is no first one on the scene—be it even some god. There is no host, no guest, no hostage. There where there is a first one on the scene, there can be no peace. No matter how gracious, how accommodating, how welcoming the first one on the scene might be, any and all who were to come after would in some way be usurpers, intruders, interlopers.

Measure-Taking

Before looking up from the field opened and cleared, before looking beyond the field opened and cleared—our upward glances passing aloft toward the sky and the divinities, thus spanning the between of earth and sky—before *this* between was measured out for dwelling, there was another between, another span, another dimension measured out for our dwelling. This is the between and toward of caring. It is in and through caring that we are first brought together, bringing us to belong with one another and to the earth—and it is thus that we are brought into dwelling. We dwell by tending toward one another, by spanning the dimension that stretches between us—and, in doing so, sharing in opening a world not only in which we can live but within which all-that-is can find a place into which it is admitted. This spanning does not cover a distance or overcome some void. Rather, the spanning of this between is a tending-toward that deepens, fecundates, and makes more profound the tending-between.

Through and within such caring there is a measure-taking. This is not an upward-looking measure-taking that would stretch between earth and sky, but a measure-taking that stretches between one and an other. If there is earth and sky here, it is in a sharing of breath, a sharing of life, a flowing of nourishment. For before the sky comes to stand above our heads, there is a sharing of air and of breath between us—a sharing in which we are preserved and protected. And before the earth comes to be beneath our feet, there is a sharing of nourishment—a sharing of the flow of life proper to no one, but which is shared out amongst us. If there are divinities here, they are not of or in the sky, but circulate in the breath and nourishment within, between, and toward one and an other.

[If humans, as humans, have always measured themselves with and against some divinity, some godhead—and such a claim is far from assured—this is not to say that they have measured themselves against the heavens or the heavenly. Before the divinities ascend into the heavens, they dwell with us, within us, between us.]

◆ ◆ ◆

The measure of this caring is a measure of the world. This means, first, that this measure is of *this* world. It does not transcend this world—rather, it belongs to it. But that the measure of this caring is a measure of the world also means that it measures this world. This world and all within the world, including the divine, is measured out within the tending-between and tending-toward of caring.

Caring: the place and occasion of all measure, and hence all value.

The Belonging Together of Between and Toward

Every between implies a toward, every toward a between. The two belong together. There is not first a between and then its spanning. The between and the spanning of the between belong together.

Although caring is both a tending-between and a tending-toward, this belonging-together is not always manifest.

At times, it is primarily as a tending-toward that caring manifests itself—tending-between remaining largely hidden, even though any tending-toward presupposes a between in which a movement toward might take place. Love is at times mistakenly taken to be a tending-toward in which the between is reduced to a minimum. But even in love, indeed, particularly in love, tending toward one another implies a tending-between. The nurturing of one is a nurturing of the other.

At other times, it is primarily as a tending-between that caring shows itself—tending-toward remaining largely hidden, even though every tending-between is simultaneously a tending-toward. The step back that clears and provides room for the other to pass is at times mistakenly taken to be a tending-between in which the toward is reduced to a minimum. But even in the step back, indeed, particularly in the step back, there is simultaneously a step toward. The nurturing of one is a nurturing of the other.

Erring-With

Our com-position is a trans-position. The *trans-* indicates simultaneously a movement across as well as a movement with—a movement across because a movement with, a movement with as a movement across.

[A movement with, a movement across—with, across what? or whom?

The differences between what and whom are to be thought in terms of this *with* and *across* rather than the other way around. The differences between whom and what, as well as their meanings, remain undecided. Thus it would be premature to assume that this trans-position is to be thought in terms of a *what* or a *That* into which we are trans-posed. It may well be that we are trans-posed with others prior to any trans-position into . . . —but the nature of these others is yet unknown, and perhaps unknowable.

Perhaps our most pressing question is not "What is called thinking?" but "Who calls me to care—and in caring calls (upon) me to think?"]

That our com-position is a trans-position indicates that it is an erring—and, more specifically, an erring-with (one another). To err is to go astray, to go across. To err is to wander out of bounds. To err-with one another is to wander in wonder with one another, to wander in wonder before one another. It is our way of way-making (together).

◆ ◆ ◆

Caring is that essential agreement between one another from out of which words might emerge. Caring is the opening in which the beings around us might appear. We are inclined toward one another such that this inclination can appear, be thought, given voice. That is, we are inclined toward one another in the manner of tending-toward one another through which there is a world between us.

[It is through and within—that is, on the ground of—that inexplicable way of erring-with one another called tending-between and tending-toward that there can unfold, among other things, the relation between Being and human nature.]

[Caring can be said to "hold together" differing and deferring. Within the tending-between and tending-toward of caring there is differing and deferring. The "holding together" of differing and deferring within caring is a holding apart as held together. Neither differing nor deferring is absolute, final. Rather, they play within, they are the play of the tending-between and tending-toward of caring. And if caring itself is to be thought (and is only thinkable) in terms of differing and deferring—the "terms" of caring differing from one another, their relation being one of deferral—this is not to say that caring presupposes differing and deferring, but that thinking presupposes differing and deferring. Differing and deferring, however, presuppose the thanking of caring.]

Caring: A Poietic Sharing

Human being: a com-position pregnant with expectation.

In sharing, we share in the origin of all things. That is, we share in the sharing forth of all that is. Thus, this origin does not lie in some more or less remote past—our task then being to recover this past. Rather, this origin shares itself forth, is shared forth, at every moment. It is a miracle in which we can share at every moment. The origin of all things is no zero-point origin; no point of singularity folded back and closed upon itself such that it would be its own foundation and origin, such that its unfolding would then be the unfolding of history and the world. The singularity of origin, like all singularity, cannot be dissociated from the com-posing of all that is. The singularity of origin is the com-posing of all that is.

Yet to give voice to that sharing in which all things share is no easy task, despite the pervasiveness with which this sharing surrounds, runs through, and sustains all that is. Nor is it easy to let that sharing be seen, despite its being everywhere. Nevertheless, in our more awakened moments we find—or rather lose—ourselves in its continual unfolding.

With regard to this sharing, it is not a question of imitating nature, of reproducing or representing that which is given to experience by way of nature, but of participating in, sharing in the very act by which nature spontaneously brings-forth. Our sharing: poietic bringing-forth—not merely imitating nature, but rather sharing in the sharing forth of nature.

Within the tending-between and tending-toward of caring, we can share in sharing in (a) new way(s)—i.e., meeting, dwelling, loving.

Our greatest poietic accomplishments: caring, meeting, dwelling, loving.

Caring: For Memory: The Gathering of Thought

Thinking originally means thanking—that is, memory, the gathering that recalls. Thinking as thanking points us toward what is most thought-provoking—that is, what is most thank-provoking. Most thank-provoking is caring, through and within which all for which we might be thankful can appear.

That thinking originally means thanking indicates to us that the essential nature of thinking is not determined by the presence of what is present, but instead by that caring through and within which the presence of what is present can be shared, and in being shared unfold.

Where some would seek thought and thinking, others undertake that caring out of which all thought can unfold; a caring that exceeds thought. Thinking remains but one possibility within caring—and if all caring implies a thinking, it does so as a mother implies a child.

◆ ◆ ◆

Thought is indeed in need of memory, the gathering of thought. And this gathering of thought, as a devotion, a steadfast concentrated abiding with one another and the earth, is in turn in need of an opening—an opening for . . . , an opening to . . . . This is an opening through and within which this gathering can gather, can take place. There is abiding only through and within some opening. That is, abiding is an opening, and abiding takes place within an opening. And this opening is, in turn, in need of caring, that tending-between and tending-toward through which the open opens, through and within which we belong with one another and the earth.

Prior to the gathering of thought there is a sharing of thought—a sharing forth of thought in the com-position of one with another that is articulated through and around tending-between and tending-toward. Sharing (as caring) is the groundless ground of memory, the gathering of thought. Memory rests upon our sharing through caring. And hence, it is caring that engenders, that brings forth thinking.

Recollection and representation are ways of attending to all-that-is—to situations, to others, to things. But these ways of attending presuppose the tending-between and tending-toward of caring. Thus, whatever recollection is necessary in order for "nature" to take form as a world, for it to be able to be represented and worked over is "accomplished" as caring.

◆ ◆ ◆

Memory as steadfast concentrated abiding is not limited to staying with what is past, but abiding with all-that-is.

Memory is the way in which we are inclined toward all-that-is. This way of being inclined rests upon and grows out of our tending-between and tending-toward one another. It is not within our control. Nor is it enacted by us. Rather, we are dis-posed (that is, trans-posed) within and through this inclination. Memory is thus com-posed, between us, prior to being a gathering of all that a heart holds in present being. For whatever a heart can hold in present being must first be shared between us, shared forth through and within a tending-between and tending-toward that reaches out and opens.

Not until history is shared can it be given. In and through sharing, history unfolds.

Sharing Distinctions

In bringing forth distinctions we share in the sharing forth of all-that-is. That is, our distinctions are performative—and, as performative, contingent.

It is not only this world that emerges in our sharing in the sharing forth of all-that-is, but also all ways of understanding the world as being discriminated into "this" or "that."

To know a thing is to know its com-position. Our knowledge is thus always proximate—for each thing's com-position is without limit. There are as many ways to know a thing as there are positions from which its com-position might be known. To know a thing is itself a position—a position that thereby enters into the com-position of things. The dream of a knowledge that would not be proximate is the dream of a knowledge beyond all positions. If our everyday ways of knowing things—of which science is but one—make it appear as if there is one privileged position, or some privileged way of reducing all difference between positions, this testifies more to the poverty of our awareness and our imagination than to the way things are.

Despite its apparent universality, contemporary science arises out of a particular kind of concern, a particular way of approaching the world and the things of the world. Although one of the advantages of treating things in the manner of science is that it suggests the possibility of complete knowledge, science remains as naïve as that everyday concern out of which it grows. This is not to impugn its efficacy but to question its comprehensiveness. For it does not comprehend that everyday way of understanding things that finds itself involved in advance with the things of this world.

◆ ◆ ◆

Because our sharing distinctions is always proximate, and hence incomplete, our being-with is a witnessing, a bearing witness.

Maternal Caring

There is a maternal caring that gives, receives, exchanges. Yet such caring is not reducible to giving, receiving, exchanging. Rather, it participates, it shares, in each. To think the maternal in terms of giving and the gift is to limit and restrict its sharing in the sharing forth of all-that-is. Nevertheless, this maternal caring is in no way pure, is in no way a care free from interest. It is always already caught up in giving and taking. Yet there are more or less accomplished ways of maternal caring—a more or less implying an ethos, an ethics.

This caring: a sharing of flesh, of blood, of breath—of life. And yet not reducible to an exchange of matter, a working upon that which is sensible; not reducible to a material or maternal overflowing. The sensible, matter, has always already been spiritualized in this sharing. Infused with breath, matter is moved, life brought forth, growth nurtured, sustained. Inspired and enthused, matter is endowed with soul.

A sharing between (them): of flesh, of blood, of breath; a sharing that is not equal but is no less a sharing for this; a sharing not reducible to division, to distribution; a sharing beyond measure, beyond rank. A sharing in which there is an indistinct proximity, a proximity destroyed in the giving and receiving of gifts, in the drawing up of sides, in the calculation of debts.

There is no debt of life here—unless it is a debt to, but also a debt shared with, all that shares in life. That is, a debt to, a debt shared with all-that-is. And although it may be true that we cannot pay back our mothers—in kind or otherwise—this is true of all with whom we share and all from whom we receive.

This caring: shared forth before there is anyone there to share in this sharing, to receive what is given. It is through the care of the mother that there comes to be one who can share, receive, and perhaps in turn give—or fail in all this by appropriating as his or her own what can only be shared.

The sharing forth of all-that-is precedes any maternal care. That is, there is a passing *between* one *and* the other before any passing *from* one *to* another. Hence, this maternal caring is not an ontological ground—or, if it is or insofar as it is, it shares in this with all-that-is. That is, maternal caring shares with all-that-is in the sharing forth of each one.

◆ ◆ ◆

This sharing of life, of breath, of blood is taken over and taken up in the building of cultivation and erection.

Maternal caring nurtures. To nurture is to cherish and protect and preserve. This nurturing is not reducible to a building that "only takes care"—tending a growth that ripens into its fruit of its own accord. And while this nurturing does not make some thing—like a temple or a ship, for example—it does not merely watch over what might unfold on its own.

That is to say, such caring is a manner of dwelling upon the earth; a manner of dwelling that is more primordial than that dwelling which involves building as cultivating or building as the raising up of edifices. It still remains to be thought in what ways these manners of building—the cultivation of soil, of the vine and the raising up of edifices—depend upon maternal caring. It still remains to be thought in what ways these manners of dwelling are restrictions and modulations of maternal caring—mere possibilities however habitual they have become, which is to say that they are not the entirety of our dwelling, our ethos.

We have only just begun to fathom that maternal care not circumscribed within the closure of our agri-culture.

Meeting

In caring for the earth, Epimetheus and Pandora met again and again for the first time. Cherishing that wonder between them, they shared in the mystery that surrounds and sustains. In drawing near to one another, they participated again and again in that sharing through which the mystery that surrounds and sustains might attain voice and body, appearing and being heard. Again and again they renewed the tending-between and tending-toward in which the wonder of the world might come forth. Preparing themselves to reclaim—and to be reclaimed by—the mystery that precedes the world, sharing in its silence, they drew near to one another again and again.

Wonder of wonders, wonder upon wonder: that one and an other can draw near to each other *as* other to each other.

To Meet: With Care

In the tending-between and tending-toward of caring, there is place and occasion for the drawing near of each one *as* other to each other. To draw near to one another as other to each other is to meet with one another.

The tending-between and tending-toward of caring can occur without those drawing near to one another meeting *as* other to each other. In meeting, each draws near to each *as* other. Thus, for one to draw near to an other as other is not yet for one and an other to meet—although such drawing near may be on the way to meeting.

◆ ◆ ◆

It is possible—and perhaps even worthwhile—to draw near to an other without that other drawing near to one. It is possible—and perhaps even worthwhile—to reverence and respect an other without this reverence or respect being mutual, without this reverence or respect being shared. It is possible—and perhaps even worthwhile—to give and receive, to give and take, and even to exchange.

And yet, however worthwhile it may be, such one-sided drawing near is not to meet. It remains a way of caring, without this caring unfolding in a meeting.

Meeting is not something that one can accomplish by oneself.

◆ ◆ ◆

The drawing near of meeting is rooted in the tending-between and tending-toward of caring. Rooted in caring, it nonetheless can rise above this ground without ever leaving it. Rooted in caring, meeting is held within and through caring. Indeed, it can be called an articulation of caring, an unfolding and refolding of caring, a joining and gathering of caring.

Drawing Near: Spanning the Between

The drawing near of meeting is a mutual spanning of the between, a mutual drawing toward one another *as* other. This spanning, this drawing toward is simultaneously a being-drawn-toward.

To span in this way is not to reduce or eliminate. It is to safeguard, to hold together. The spanning of the between, the drawing toward of one and another in meeting does not in any way obliterate or reduce the between. Indeed, the spanning intensifies the between—letting it, helping it become ever more profound. Hence, it is a mutual caring for the between.

◆ ◆ ◆

Meeting is not simply the consequence of two or more wills, two or more intentionalities deciding to draw near to one another. It is not within the power of any will, of any intentionality, or any collection of wills or intentionalities, to bring about the meeting of two or more. Indeed, it often happens that the will or intention to meet forecloses the opportunity to meet by arranging things in advance—by no longer or not yet drawing near with an other *as* other to each other, but instead by approaching an other as the object of will or intention. Although it is not within the power of any will or intentionality to bring about a meeting, the will or intention to meet can attend to and nurture an openness, a willingness, a certain hope—which is not to say an anticipation—for meeting.

We can prepare ourselves for our meeting—even though there is no preparation that can secure a meeting for us.

Neither the will nor the intention to meet is necessary or sufficient for meeting.

As a *mutual* drawing toward and being-drawn-toward one another as other to each other, meeting is shared, held in common. On the basis of this common ground, the drawing toward of meeting can become reciprocal, alternating back and forth *from* one *to* another. But such reciprocity presupposes the being in common of a mutuality shared between each who meets.

That is to say, the mutuality of meeting is not reducible to or equivalent to some form of reciprocity.

That meeting is shared, held in common is not to say that each shares in the same way, that each share is equivalent to every other. There is neither equivalence nor non-equivalence in meeting. Rather, there is a harmonization to which each contributes; a harmonization in which each through sharing with the other(s) enhances the others(s) without sacrifice and without loss of singularity; a harmonization in which each shares with the other(s) without being dissolved into a unity or totality.

Each draws near along a singular way.

Each makes way for others in a singular manner.

The drawing near of meeting can be said to be a non-synchronizable diachrony. As such, the drawing near of meeting cannot be thematized, held within consciousness, become an object of knowledge.

Although it is non-synchronizable, this diachrony can be harmonized.

The drawing near of meeting is a mutual intertwining of hearts-and-minds. As such, it is not a cognitive act. Nor is it a form of recognition, or even acknowledgement, insofar as this might reduce the mystery of one for an other.

Sharing in the Mystery

The mutual spanning of the between is a way of being-*with*-one-another *as* other to each other that draws and is drawn further into the irreducible mystery of each one and the irreducible mystery that forever stands between each and all. Such drawing and being drawn shares in bringing forth the mystery of each and all, the mystery between each and all.

This bringing forth is not a bringing forth into some bright light of manifestation and examination. It is not a bringing forth that would dispel the mystery in the bright light of concern, the bright light of evidence. Rather, this mystery is brought forth as concealed—and in this way the mystery grows more profound, more fecund.

In the drawing near of each other as other, the irreducible singularity of each one is in no way diminished. Indeed, it grows with the mutual approach.

◈ ◈ ◈

The mutual spanning of the between is a sharing in the mystery that belongs to no one but that binds each and all, that binds each to all.

◈ ◈ ◈

In meeting, we stand in wonder before the irreducible mystery of each other. And yet there is a tendency for this wonder to become lost in curiosity. Lost in curiosity, meeting is no longer shared but instead is taken as given. In this way, meeting becomes something to be explained—meeting is taken as given for explanation, meeting is taken as that which is to be explained.

Explanation would result in the disappearance of what could arouse curiosity. Upon being explained, the curiosity (of meeting) would be dissolved. In this way, the curiosity (of meeting) would have a beginning and an end.

There are myriad benefits in wonder becoming lost in curiosity. But meeting is not one of these goods.

The wonder of meeting can deepen into a certainty—but this certainty in no way dispels or allays the wonder of meeting.

The mystery is not some nut to be cracked. It is a seed to be planted and cared for. This is a cultivation other than that of agri-culture.

The challenge in meeting is not to dispel the mystery, but to share in its fecundation.

The Proximity of Meeting

To span the between is not to cross a distance that can be quantitatively measured. No exertion of the legs can bring two (or more) nearer to one another. Thus, the spanning of the between is not the reduction of some physical distance.

The drawing near of meeting does not result in a physical proximity. The proximity of meeting is not the measure of an interval that would narrow in the drawing near of meeting. Nor is it the narrowing of an interval that could end in coincidence. Rather, in the proximity of meeting, the interval grows, deepens, becomes more profound.

In the proximity of meeting, there is contact—but not coincidence or conjuncture, for this would imply that the meeting of one *and* another, of one *with* another forms a totality constituted through addition, thereby destroying the relation, the relating of one *and* another, of one *with* another.

The proximity of meeting is tangible. It has a vibrating restlessness—*sensed* in the sharing of breath, the quivering of lips, the trembling of hands, the averting of eyes, the scent of another's skin. But this tangibility is not visible to an outside observer. It is *revealed* only to those who are touched, only to those who share in meeting.

The proximity of meeting is an exposure of one *and* another, of one *with* another—and hence it can be an exposure of one *to* another. The exposure of meeting is a sharing of fragility. It presupposes a relaxation if not a dropping away or dissolution of that armor with which we are sheltered (and shelter ourselves) from others, from the world, and even from ourselves. In the exposure of meeting, each is turned "inside out" in such a way that the distinction between outer and inner can disappear.

The Possibility of Meeting

If, to meet, each must draw near to each other as other, it would seem unlikely that those without the possibility to approach some one or some thing *as* other would share in meeting. And yet, who can say whether an other is (un)able to meet? For it is not within any one's power to preclude an other—a child, an animal, a stone; the demented, the dead—from meeting. One can erect or place barriers in the way of an other, but this is not to preclude an other's ability to meet with others, however unlikely such meeting may thus become. Yet one can keep one's self from meeting with others.

No more than the foundation of the self is to be found in the self, is the foundation of meeting to be found in (the wills, the intentionalities, the powers of) those who meet.

Meeting is not within any one's power.

◆ ◆ ◆

There is a freedom that does not imply autonomy or any power of the self, but an irreducible mystery over which no one can exercise any control; an untouchability that would exceed any grasp, be it mental or physical.

This freedom does not consist in spontaneity. Nor does it consist in some power or ability. It is not Promethean, but Epimethean.

◆ ◆ ◆

In and through the wonder of meeting, possibilities of being with one another as other to each other—that is, shared possibilities—are disclosed.

With each one drawing near along a singular way, meeting is an opening-through-joining of new horizons, new prospects, new ventures. This opening-through-joining discloses new possibilities of being-with-one-another.

Such disclosure, like all disclosure, is a com-posure. That is, this disclosure is a putting together, a being put together. It is a further intertwining of hearts-and-minds, a further intertwining of joint destinies—not in the sense of a fate that compels but as a being-sent-along-the-way-together.

In the intertwining of destinies, each comes to stand caringly, thoughtfully with others. This standing with others is a going-along-the-way together. It is a sharing of life.

It happens that each meets with him- or herself in meeting with others. And in meeting with oneself an exclusive concern with one's own death can come about.

One way of being-with-one-another is to anticipate. And this anticipation can take many forms, from concerns with regard to common projects to an exclusive concern with one's own death—for even within such exclusive concern, one is still with others, even if in an impoverished way. In all anticipation, there is a disclosure of possibilities for those so disposed. Yet the disclosure of possibilities in anticipation is a possibility made possible through meeting. From the wonder of meeting, anticipation can be said to fall out.

On the groundless ground of wonder, we can come to anticipate and to remember.

In and through meeting, the finitude of each one is realized. This finitude is not found in the being-towards-death of each one but in being-*with*-others. In and through meeting, we engage and are engaged in ways of being with one another in and through which an exclusive concern with one's own possibilities of being would dissolve—not into a lostness or dispersion in others, but in the wonder of sharing life caringly and thoughtfully with others.

What is disclosed in meeting is not one's ownmost possibilities but the possibilities of being-with-others in which life and death are shared and have sense—that is, meaning and direction. In meeting, we come to see that we are not the whole, for if we were we would not be able to meet with another as other. And furthermore we come to see that we cannot accomplish on our own either the disclosure of meeting or the fulfillment in word, in deed of meeting.

In and through meeting, we come to see that our being-with-others will never fail us. We will never be, even in the moment of death, without others.

This lesson can be neglected, even forgotten—if it is not commemorated now and again.

A Place and Occasion of Wonder: The Time and Space of Meeting

The time of meeting is a time of awe. It is awe-full.

Wrapped in wonder, meeting unfolds a new temporal order. That is, with meeting there is a renewal of time, of possibility.

This renewal of time does not take place in any given time. It is a sharing forth of time in and through which the world is brought forth anew.

◆ ◆ ◆

To go to meeting is to wander into a wilderness—the wilderness of the between. To wander into a wilderness is to surrender to the will of the place and occasion. To go to meeting is thus to put oneself at risk—the risk of not knowing with whom one will meet or what will come out of the meeting; but also the risk of failing to meet, the risk of one's laying oneself open not being shared.

To go to meeting, to wander into a wilderness calls for courage, the courage to be fragile.

◆ ◆ ◆

We come to meet with one another in the clearing that stretches between us, a clearing that belongs to no one but to which each belongs. This clearing may be more or less open—but it is open nonetheless. Thus, even in the domestication of our being-with-one-another—even in the anticipation and arrangement of our being-with-one-another—meeting, however unlikely, can still unfold.

To wander in wonder (before the mystery of each other) is to tread upon a groundless ground.

Meeting: In the Moment

Meeting is not continuous with the time of history. Thus, we meet without this meeting taking place within the time of any (universal) history.

Furthermore, the temporal unfolding of history, of historical time, presupposes that of meeting.

In every meeting, there is a suspending of time, a diremption of time. To all appearances, this suspension is merely relative and is quickly recoupable. And yet . . .

This is also to say that memory and anticipation will only take us so far along the way to meeting.

Within a meeting, there is neither memory nor anticipation insofar as they objectify or arrange in advance or place within a totality. Yet we can go to and from meeting pregnant with anticipation, pregnant with memory.

It can be rather difficult to meet with those with whom we are familiar. Often, and perhaps unavoidably, we carry assumptions and expectations of them—and these assumptions and expectations can burden us with a weight that inhibits our *being-with-others*. Our very intimacy can bind us so closely together that we no longer, or only with great difficulty, perceive that distance between us in which we can meet. Instead it is the stranger, the one who comes from without, from beyond, who draws near. Unburdened by assumptions and expectations, we can make our way toward one another. There stands between us that distance through and across which we can draw near to one another.

◆ ◆ ◆

Meeting unfolds in a dimension of its own where it has meaning. This dual unfolding of meeting and its meaning is otherwise than a temporal unfolding belonging to some history.

There is a surplus of meaning in each meeting that exceeds and eludes every appropriative grasping that would fix the meeting and its meaning within some history.

We meet in the blink of an eye—in a time outside of time.

◆ ◆ ◆

The moment of meeting is not one of resolution but one of surrender.

Meeting: Always for the First Time

As a diremption of time—a suspending of the duration, of the continuity that has preceded it—each meeting is an absolute beginning. In meeting, there is a renewal of time, of the unfolding of time, of that out of which time unfolds. That is, there is a renewal of caring.

Each meeting is like the birth of a child—it is a breaking in and breaking up of time; it exceeds anticipation; it is an absolute beginning; as such it is not only a breaking up of time but also a falling out of—and that from out of which falls—a new temporal order, new possibilities.

In meeting we draw near—even with old, familiar friends—again and again for the first time. In meeting, there is no giving and taking of that old musty cheese that we are.

Meeting: With-Memory

No memory can recapture our meeting. It can only be com-memorated—and thereby brought forth again and again for the first time.

Meeting can no more be remembered than birth can be remembered by the one born. It can only be commemorated.

To commemorate is to bring forth again for the first time.

Meeting: An Unfolding of Conversation

Our meeting is that from out of which every conversation unfolds and grows. To converse is to have one's being among—that is, *with*—others. It is to live with others, to dwell with others, and perhaps to love with others.

This conversation is not reducible to anything said—it exists in its saying. Saying here is not reducible to grammar, words, articulate speech. It is another way of saying caring.

Conversation, in the sense of exchanging thoughts and words, is only one possibility of meeting—even if it has for quite some time been an integral part of our meetings.

When the wonder of meeting becomes lost in curiosity, our being-with-one-another becomes lost in discursive affairs: the giving and taking of *logos*: words, reasons, accounts. Such giving and taking is not to be confused with the sharing of conversation. In this sharing, a momentous silence reigns. This silence has no end—and even our speech would be but the beginning of it.

Meeting: With: The(e): Everyday

We find ourselves forever on the way to meeting. In this sense, meeting can be said to be mundane. But to be mundane here is not to be routine, dreary, unexciting. It is in and through the mundane that we share in a world. The mundane is world-forming. It is of the world. It is that which is common, that which is held in common—that is, the world, between us.

We can meet with that which lies beyond all words in the most simple, humble, everyday realities. Everyday life itself, particularly in our relations with others, can be charged with wonder, awe, mystery.

The miracle and wonder of meeting surges forth again and again. But this miracle, this wonder can be so covered over and occluded that even the trace of meeting eludes the conscious mind.

The challenge then is to transform our everyday meetings; to overcome a lostness in ordinary ways of being-with-one-another—expectation, appropriation, curiosity, idle chatter; ordinary ways that occlude the extra-ordinary character of every meeting.

The challenge is to make ourselves worthy to meet. The challenge is to remain open and ready to draw and be drawn together.

Meeting: With: The Divine

In every meeting, we meet with the divine.

In every meeting, there is a disclosing of the mystery of each one and the mystery that forever stands between each and all. Such disclosure is a disclosure of the divine, a disclosure in which the mystery is revealed as concealed.

With every failure to meet, the divine withdraws further and further into a concealment without this concealment showing itself.

[It has been said with some justification that God is dead. But gods die peculiar deaths.

They die in our failure to meet. They die in our turning away from the mystery as mystery. They die in becoming transparent.

Still, every meeting is a resurrection of the divine.]

Dwelling

Epimetheus and Pandora wandered over the face of the earth. And everywhere they wandered, there they dwelled. Erring now here, now there, their home was always with them. Threading the valleys, crossing the plains, climbing high mountains: their sojourning was a dwelling, their dwelling a sojourning.

Naked, unshod, unbedded, unarmed. Yet not without a home. Open, fragile—held within sharing and caring, able to dwell. Indeed, able to dwell because naked, unshod, unbedded, unarmed—and thus open, fragile.

Dwelling: Residing in Caring

The care through and within which we are brought into the world is the first and enduring place and occasion for our dwelling. Held within and supported by the care of others, we are cradled and comforted. In their hearts and in their hands, we are embraced and sustained.

Our dwelling resides in this caring. It is this caring that first allows dwelling to be dwelling. It is this caring that really lets us dwell. We attain to dwelling through caring. And caring, which lets us dwell, is a kind of sharing. Dwelling here is not a mode of maintaining oneself or being at home with oneself, nor is it a site of power, of being-able-to . . . . It is not even the manner in which we are upon the earth. Before it is a site, a physical space, situated in the world or upon the earth, it is an attending in which one and the other are first brought forth and brought together, brought forth in being brought together. It is a touching and being touched by the other in the distance of proximity. A touching in which there are not yet fixed boundaries. A touching immersed in the elemental mystery that surrounds.

In this dwelling, we do not persist through spaces by virtue of our stay among things and locations. For in this caring-dwelling, it is not things that lie

71

near to us. It is not things that gather to themselves earth and sky, mortals and divinities. In this caring-dwelling nothing, no-thing—not even language?—has come to stand between those who dwell together. Before any thing comes to stand between, there is the stretching between of caring in which (at least) two draw and are drawn near to one another. Through and within caring, dwelling unfolds, stretches out, rises up, and blossoms.

On the basis of this dwelling there can be the cultivation of the vine, the tilling of soil, the raising up of buildings, but the dwelling that resides in caring is in no way reducible to or exhausted in these agri-cultural machinations. These agri-cultural ways of dwelling all presuppose and rest upon that dwelling that resides in caring. For before there can be any opening and clearing of the field, any settling alongside the field opened and cleared, there must be a nurturing and sustaining of body-and-soul, a nurturing and sustaining of heart-and-mind; there must first be a standing upright in body-and-soul, an edification of body-and-soul that precedes the various ways of building peculiar to agri-culture.

[This edification, this raising up of body-and-soul, is in no way limited to the raising of children. Indeed, the edification of children presupposes a prior edification of those who dwell together—a dwelling together within which a raising up of children irreducible to a biological unfolding is possible.]

The agri-cultural life which is commonly praised and regarded as successful is but one kind. Why should we exaggerate any one kind at the expense of others?

In attending to dwelling, we come to understand that:
1. Dwelling resides in caring.
2. Caring is a tending between and a tending toward.
3. Dwelling as sharing and caring can unfold into the dwelling that cultivates growing things and the dwelling that erects buildings.

The Sharing of Dwelling

Together we dwell—*with* one another. *With* one another, through and within the sharing and caring between us, dwelling is brought forth and sustained. Dwelling is not *mine*, not *yours*—nor is it simply *ours*. We belong to dwelling before "it" belongs to us. In dwelling, we belong, together.

This is to say that dwelling cannot be given, taken, exchanged. It can only be shared. Dwelling con-sists in its being shared. Con-sisting in its being shared, dwelling is not and cannot be accomplished once and for all, presented as some finished product. It is forever ongoing, shared between us.

Shared between us, one cannot give (a) dwelling to another. It is not one's to give. It is not among the things that can be traded in this way. In dwelling, there can be giving, taking, exchange, but only because dwelling is first shared between. This sharing, this dwelling *with* one another, precedes and sustains the back and forth—the *to*, *for*, or *from* standing between one and another—of exchange, of giving, of receiving.

◆ ◆ ◆

This sharing of dwelling is a commemoration of caring, of meeting. Dwelling is this commemoration.

The Home as a Manner of Dwelling

In dwelling, there is between us a nearness that does not efface all that separates us while drawing us together. That is, there is a home. And to dwell is to be at home. The home is not a site of imminence. It is not a site of fusion or oneness. It is not a domesticated safe haven. The hearth is the curved space-time of joint solitude, of the outside drawing near. To be at home means to be at risk—(even) in the warmth of proximity. To be at home is to share in a mutual drawing near, a mutual caring with and for one another. It is something one can never do alone.

The home is not some thing among things, nor is it a collection of things. It is not a consequence of seizing and taking things into some interiority. Nor does it involve an appropriation of what lies without. To be at home is not to subsist among things or alongside others. Nor is to be at home to be distributed alongside others within a common physical space. Rather, it is to be with one another, to mutually tend the between and toward of caring. It is to mutually span the dimension that stretches between us. It is a sharing of breath, a sharing of nourishment, a sharing of life—all of which imply a certain proximity. This is the proximity of the hearth, the proximity of the table—and such proximity is first and foremost a relation between us, not a physical site.

The first hearth: the breast upon which we suckle, upon which we are suckled. The first table: the hand with which we are held, caressed. Thus, neither breast nor hand is reducible to a mute nature. Each conveys the heart-and-mind of one who cares.

The home is rooted in such caring—not as a house rests upon its foundation, standing erect upon stone and mortar, but as a seed is rooted in a nourishing soil. This nourishing soil is the hearts-and-minds of those who care with and for one another. Thus, no home is attached to one site, tied down to a particular location. Rather, it is bound with and to the hearts-and-minds of those who care with and for one another. The home is not *hers*, not *his*—perhaps it is not even *ours*. We belong to the home before "it" belongs to us. In the home, we belong, together.

Dwelling: In the Openness of the Home

In the home, there is an openness—an openness between those who dwell together as well as an openness extended to those who draw near from farther away. The openness of the home is not yet hospitality or welcome, even if it provides the place and occasion for them. That is to say, openness is a necessary but not a sufficient condition for hospitality and welcome. For hospitality and welcome require a mutual opening between and toward those who draw near.

This openness of the home offers the place and occasion for meeting with the stranger. It is into this openness of the home that the stranger arrives with a startling unexpectedness. Such an arrival is a miracle—it is to be wondered at. The startling unexpectedness of the stranger is awe-some. It leaves us awe-struck. The stranger, like the newly born child, is the singular, the unique—before whom lies no precedent.

It is within and into the openness of the home that the stranger can be received and welcomed. Such welcoming, like all welcoming, does not happen straightaway. Welcoming is not merely an invitation across a threshold. It involves making way and making room in one's heart-and-mind for others. It calls for and calls forth the unfolding of a time between us—a shared time in which there might be a giving and taking, call and response, exchange.

A home without such openness, a home unable to receive a stranger would not be a home. A home cannot be closed to the arrival of the stranger without ceasing to be a home.

[In birth, we witness the miracle of change, the arrival of the startlingly unexpected, the wondrously unforeseen. And this is a miracle taking place at every moment. It is everywhere and everywhen—even in death, if only we have eyes to see and ears to hear.]

The openness of the home, like all openness, is neither infinite nor absolute. Nor is it unconditional. Indeed, dwelling and the home can be said to be a joint articulation of our finitude. As such, no dwelling, no home can guarantee that no matter how bad things become there will be some haven that welcomes and protects us from what threatens. There is no such guarantee. There is, at best, a promise to be renewed again and again.

Proximity and Distance: Within the Home

In the openness of the home, there is proximity and distance. That is to say, within the home there is no fusion, no homogenization, no totalization. Nor is there a merging together into a uniform distancelessness. The singularity of each one is not dissolved or drowned in a homogenizing sameness. Proximity and contact—and the distance, the standing apart, the between they imply—are maintained, and indeed are deepened and become more fecund.

To dwell together is to care for oneself and for others. And the home is a place and occasion for such care, a place and occasion to prepare room for one another, a place and occasion to recover and renew the body-and-soul of each and all. This preparing room for others is a making and letting be that does not arrange everything in advance, but a leaving open for the other or others to reside therein. Thus, the room prepared for each is a room to which one belongs as well as a room which belongs to one.

There is indeed a gathering together in our dwelling, a gathering together indicated in our drawing near. Yet this is a gathering together that lets each lie in their proper dispersion. This is the systole and diastole of dwelling.

In dwelling, each—person, thing, word—is let to lie in their proper dispersion. And this is no easy task. Nevertheless, to dwell together, within the home, this is what must happen. Each must learn to step back, to respect that nearness that does not efface all that separates us while drawing us together. Each must learn to step back and make way for others. Now this stepping back and making way can only be done because we are already together, with one another. Stepping back and making way for one another are thus ways of being with one another, ways of attending to and for one another. In this way, each—person, thing, word—can find a fitting place through letting each and all lie in their proper dispersion.

◆ ◆ ◆

In the proximity and distance of the home, we meet again and again for the first time.

Dwelling and/as Exposure

We come into the world naked, unshod, unbedded, and unarmed—that is, we come into the world exposed. And there is no covering that can cover over this, our exposure. We are not just exposed now and then. Rather, our essential nature is exposure.

Our dwelling does not and ought not eliminate this exposure. To dwell together is to be exposed with and to one another—that is, to lay open and be laid open with and to one another. To dwell together is to share our exposure, to share our fragility, to share our nakedness. It is a mutual disclosure of *who* we are.

Our dwelling together is a standing-with-one-another—that is, our dwelling together is a com-position. Our standing-with-one-another does not result from our being placed alongside or in the vicinity of one another. To-stand-with-one-another is to stand *before* one another—not in the sense of "standing in advance of" or merely "standing in front of" as a rock stands in front of an entrance but in the sense of "facing one another." To face one another is to be exposed with and to one another. Thus, our composition is an exposition, our composure an exposure. To be with one another, to stand with one another is to incline and to be inclined toward one another.

Dwelling does not shelter us from the elements, nor does it shelter us from uncertainty or from danger. Dwelling is not a foothold in that which surrounds and sustains us: a field we cultivate, a sea in which we fish and moor our boat, a forest in which we cut wood. We do not plunge from dwelling into some elemental outside. Nor does dwelling provide us in any simple way with a refuge from all that is uncanny, from all that discomfits us. Even in dwelling, there is no evading the strange and the stranger, there is no evading birth and death.

In dwelling, we are exposed with and to others. And to be thus exposed is to be exposed to the future, to be exposed to death—what is, perhaps too hastily and too thoughtlessly, called our own death, as well as the deaths of others. The attempt to eliminate or overcome our exposure, the attempt to make the home free from danger and fear, runs the risk of foreclosing our relation to the other, to the future, to death.

In seeking to reduce, if not eliminate, danger and fear, the attempt is made to close off the home, to fix its boundaries, to police its borders; to secure the home by determining and knowing in advance who or what is coming; to cover and arrange all that lies between (a tending toward that can variously obscure, cover, or arrange in advance what lies between). Securing the entrances and exits of the home—and by extension of what might be thought of as a homeland—the attempt is made to determine in advance who is friend and who is foe. And, of course, this presupposes not only that it is possible to determine who is friend and who is foe but that it is possible to do so from a distance and in advance of their arrival. We must know in advance who and what is coming. We must be able to anticipate the future—that is, to know in advance, to make the future present in advance of its arrival.

And yet, can there be such anticipation of the future? Is not the future the coming of the startlingly unexpected, the unknown—indeed, the unknowable and that which cannot be expected? The desire to know who and what comes, and to be secure in this knowing, is a desire to live without others, a desire to live without a future—and a desire to live without death. It is a desire to live within a home closed off to the other as other, closed off to the other as one who arrives, who draws near—or perhaps departs—with a startling unexpectedness. It is thus a desire to live within a home closed off to the future. And yet, is a home possible—and more importantly, desirable—under such conditions? What must the home be such that it could exist closed off to the other as other, closed off to the future, closed off to death?

The Fragility of Dwelling

Naked, unshod, unbedded, unarmed. Yet not without a home. Open, fragile—held within sharing and caring, able to dwell. Indeed, able to dwell because naked, unshod, unbedded, unarmed—and thus open, fragile.

The home is shared and is a sharing between those who are fragile. And the home itself is fragile. Unlike the house, the function of which is to cover and conceal—and thereby protect us from what and who lies beyond its walls—the home is a privileged place and occasion in which we uncover and reveal ourselves to one another while retaining our mystery. Whereas a house may serve to secure and guarantee our physical existence, and to do so may require a solidity closed upon itself, the home, as a place and occasion of our relations with one another, is unavoidably fragile.

This fragility of the home and of our relations with one another is manifest not only in the births and deaths that take place within the home, simultaneously threatening its existence and offering to strengthen its bonds, but in all our relations with others, from the most distant to the most intimate. In all our relations with others, we are laid open and lay ourselves open. It is this laying open that is put at risk in any attempt to regulate and control the movements and actions of everyone within, around, and outside the home.

The home and all who share a home, must remain unfinished and open—open to a coming and becoming of each one. It is all too easy to suppress dwelling, to cause it to tremble. It is all too easy for one alone to attempt to appropriate and close off what can only be shared between. Although it requires two or more for a dwelling to be established, one alone can suppress a dwelling. One alone can dissolve the dwelling—not merely through some action, some will or intention, but through neglect, forgetfulness.

The home only con-sists, only holds together and is held together, in its being shared. With the disappearance or cessation of this sharing, there is no longer any home. Floors, walls, ceilings—these may remain. But the home is no longer. Consisting in its being shared, the home is forever threatened by the appropriation involved in giving, taking, exchange.

The Constancy of the Home

Despite the fragility that inheres in dwelling, there is a constancy within and around the home. The bonds of this constancy are the bonds of a shared faith—a confiding and a confidence; a sharing of faith with and in one another, a sharing of faith with and in each as well as in all that lies between. The bonds of this shared faith are the bonds of a mutual commitment and promise between those who dwell together. Such commitment and promise are not accomplished once and for all, but con-sist in being renewed again and again. It is the renewal of this shared commitment and promise that constitutes the constancy of the home. This constancy abides in the renewal of the mutual commitment and promise of those who dwell together, drawing upon the faith in and the faithfulness toward those with whom one shares a home. There is, then, in the home a fragile constancy, a constant fragility.

The bonds of this shared faith constitute the tenacity of the home. This tenacity comes not from the home being closed back upon itself or from its being closed off from others. Rather, it comes from a mutual holding open, a holding open of each one with and to others. It is through this shared faith, and the openness that faith implies, that the home can hold together through losses that destroy the physical structure in which it was formerly housed. It is around this shared faith that a warmth, the warmth of the hearth, can be enjoyed—even in a cold world. And it is by way of this shared faith that the home enjoys a supple, flexible enduring.

This tenacity is shared without diminishing—indeed, it is through being shared that the tenacity, the holding together and being held together of dwelling grows. And such tenacity dissolves the moment this sharing dissolves. That is to say, this tenacity dissolves with the loss of a shared faith and faithfulness.

In and around the home, there is an intertwining of hearts-and-minds. This intertwining of hearts-and-minds is an intertwining of mouths, of hands, of bodies; an intertwining articulated in the kissing of lips, the sharing of words, the holding of hands; an intertwining articulated in singing and dancing. It is a binding together of lives.

[It is this binding together of lives that prevents the home from being in any simple way a place of convenience or relaxation. For such intertwining is an exposure of one and another, of one with and to another. And such exposure is never without risk, whatever its rewards.]

The constancy of the home can be actualized, but cannot be materialized. Like the constancy of a faith it cannot be won once and for all, but must be renewed again and again. Hence, such constancy cannot be made present. It does not show itself in this way. It is not a property that the home possesses. It is the way, the waymaking of being at home.

Dwelling and Conversation

To dwell is to converse with one another. And to converse is to live with one another and to share thoughts with one another. Our dwelling is a conversation—a holding and being held between, a going on the way together. It is a breaking and sharing of bread, of thought, of word. It is through and around such sharing that a common hearth and a common table can come to be constituted.

This conversation is a letting each and all lie in their proper dispersion, a letting things lie in their proper dispersion, a letting words and thoughts lie in their proper dispersion. It is a sharing of thoughts, a dia-logue—not a thematization that would wrap everything up in a totality or a totalizing account.

It happens that a gulf can open up between those who dwell with one another. And the way to span, if not bridge, this gulf becomes difficult to discern. No words, no actions seem available to risk this spanning. Each word uttered sinks into the abyss; each action adds to the gulf rather than spanning it; each, rather than helping to draw together, divides.

Yet even in such circumstances, we are still with and among others—and it is because of this that our pain can be so great.

Dwelling and Community

In dwelling, we belong *with* one another—and in belonging with one another we can belong *to* and *for* one another. In other words, our dwelling can be a place and occasion for the practice of community. Like dwelling, community is something shared between us, something to which we belong rather than something we possess. It is something in which we participate, something we share and something in which we share, rather than being something that we might give, receive, exchange, possess.

To dwell together is not simply to live alongside one another. Dwelling does not come about from our being placed side by side. And, in fact, such closeness—be it biological; be it linguistic; be it local, cultural, national, etc.—can impede our approaching one another. Often, and perhaps unavoidably, we carry assumptions and expectations of those with whom we are most familiar—and these assumptions and expectations can burden us with a weight that prevents our *being-with-others*. Our very intimacy can bind us so closely together that we no longer, or only with great difficulty, perceive that distance between us in which we can meet. Instead it is the stranger—the one who comes from without, from beyond—who draws near. Unburdened by assumptions and expectations, we can make our way toward one another. There stands between us that distance through and across which we can draw near to one another.

In dwelling, the interval between us is to be maintained—indeed, it is to be deepened and made more fecund. The community of dwelling is not a homogenizing fusion in which all singularity would be erased, dissolved, drowned. It is for this reason that our dwelling together suffers when our closeness leads to forgetting that between us there are significant differences—significant differences that result from the multiplicity of our ways of signifying. It suffers when we would substitute agreement for significance and signification, forgetting that significance is a sharing of our differences, forgetting that it is such significant and signifying differences that draw us together while holding us apart. And it suffers when we forget that these differences are not to be lamented but are to be cultivated and enriched—indeed, celebrated.

Sharing our differences, we draw near with and to one another, becoming aware of the differences and the diversity between us and then creating ways of approaching one another; ways of approaching for which we still lack the words; ways of approaching that do not simply unfold naturally; ways of approaching that are not technically produced or mastered; ways of approaching that, without reducing our differences in a homogenizing sameness, allow us to hold dialogues, to share places and occasions, to bring forth together the new and the unexpected. What is brought forth and shared in this way—an indivisible whole that extends between—cannot be appropriated or mastered by any one without ceasing to be.

As a result of our failure to be with one another, we become world weary, each of us being required to bear a weight—the weight of the world—alone. But it is too difficult to bear this weight alone—it can only be borne together, in company with others. Our failure to be with one another, to bring forth worlds between us, throws us back upon ourselves, requiring us to bear a weight that in one sense can be borne together but that in another sense, in being borne together, loses its weightiness by being shared.

If there is today a trembling in our belonging, such trembling is not foreign to the nature of dwelling. To dwell is to tremble—together.

The Errance of Dwelling

At home, we wander in wonder.

Still wandering, still on the way—we are yet at home in the world. Wandering, we point in several directions, in several times, at once.

A first direction, a first time. Wandering, we are on the way toward a recovery of the home. Wandering, yet nevertheless comforted by the memory of our home. Simultaneously behind us and in front of us, the home would be the reassuring beginning and end of our journey. Having set out from the home, we seek to return to the home. Thus, still wandering, still on the way, we ask, "Are we home yet?"

A second direction, a second time. Wandering, we are on the way toward a home yet unknown, a home still to come, a home not yet brought forth into the world. Still wandering, yet nevertheless comforted by the prospect of our arrival. For upon arrival, a certain wandering would be over, the way having been crossed.

A third direction, a third time—a crossing of the preceding two. Wandering, we are on the way toward the recovery of a home still to come—a wandering without nostalgia, without a return home. A recovery not of that which would (simply) stand behind us—but a recovery of the still-to-come, of a home still to come. A home not grounded in the past—its foundations laid, its hearth fire received. But a home that opens the future, that (re)calls us to the future—a home within which we perhaps already stumble about aimlessly. A home we inhabit, in which we take shelter—without yet dwelling in it.

A fourth direction, a fourth time? We are at home in wandering. In other words, wandering, we are nevertheless at home. However improbable, such wandering is not without promise. For it indicates that the openness of wandering is not foreign or antithetical to the home and being at home. And it reminds us that to foreclose wandering, to remain within a secured enclosure, be it that of a future, is to foreclose the possibility of the home and the openness it presupposes.

Only when we wander thus do we appreciate the vastness and strangeness of our dwelling. In this wandering we must again and again learn the points of compass. Only when we wander thus do we begin to find ourselves, and realize where we are and the extent of our relations.

Loving

> The devotion of Epimetheus and Pandora for one another was an altar upon the earth. Each one's body was a pathway to the divine. Exerting themselves to the utmost, they extended themselves to one another, bringing forth between them the divine. Together they celebrated marvelous festivals of joy, their laughter blessing the earth. Together they silently smiled at their ever recurring good fortune. Together they shared their breath with one another. Together, each was to the other a rare and precious treasure. Together they brought forth between them a love that could only be shared.

Oh, the poverty of language! We wish to ring in the wisdom of love with bells, and yet all we can offer is the jingling of these common coins.

Dwelling, we are on the way to love; a love rooted within sharing and caring; a love that blossoms and bears fruit through meeting and dwelling. From the seeds of that caring which begins in wonder, a love can blossom. A fragile flower, a delicate fruit—there is no guarantee that it will ever see the light of day.

And yet, wonder of wonders, love springs forth again and again. Wonder of wonders, love is brought forth again and again. With love, our wonder deepens and grows more profound. With love, we are enveloped in the great mystery of this world.

The Language of Love

It is already too late to issue a word of caution. We have dared to speak and to write of love. Indeed, have we been speaking or writing of anything else? We have dared to make of love a theme; to treat it as an object. Yet however worthy this theme, however lofty this object, we risk bringing love low in treating it in this way. We risk wandering from the way of love. It is not fine and penetrating words that we seek but to love and to be loved, to share in love. And thus we can wander from the way of love by becoming lost in words about love, confusing love with a discourse on love. It may well be that words and the saying of words are (a part) of the way of love itself—yet this way is not limited to words, reducible to words, exhausted in words.

The way of love is a way of indirection. It meanders now here, now there. It is a gently flowing water that smoothes even the roughest rock. It carries us away. It surges forth, overflowing all the words that might contain it, define it, limit it. It eludes our grasp, eludes all that is said of it.

◆ ◆ ◆

We hesitate to remain silent, not wanting to say too little. Yet we also hesitate to speak, not wanting, simultaneously, to say too little or to say too much. And we hesitate for not all have ears to hear. Thus, our words take the form of a prayer, between us, from one and another, from one to another.

◆ ◆ ◆

The words of love we offer are not our own. They are shared between us, like all words. They are called forth in a dialogue that shares in love. They are shared in a loving talk, they are shared in a loving chorus. This sharing is a going on the way together. It is a joining of breath, a joining of voices. And these words, like love itself, do not seek to appropriate or to possess. They do not seek to confine, but to set free.

We are on the way of love, and to be on the way of love is to be on the way to love. We aspire to share in a confession of love, to share in bringing love and its profession forth (for our vows of love are indeed of a religious nature). We aspire to testify as to our love—not as disinterested spectators but as participants who share in love. We aspire not merely to speak but to sing and to be carried away with love, to bring forth love by way of poetry, by way of song. And we hope with this poietic language to share in bringing forth love, between us.

Love: Of Silence

Yet the language of love is not made of mere words. For love follows after silence. And the language of love too follows after silence. It is not simply to be found in what is said, but also in its saying.

Indeed, the love between us in no way fully reveals itself in what is said of it. For it speaks without voice, inclined otherwise than what can be said of it, inclined otherwise than what is offered up in what can be said of it. Between us, like love, the language of love can be found in the interstices of our words, in the sharing flow of their saying. In the saying shared between us, our hearts-and-minds are bound together. To be bound together in this way is to be bound by more than words and by more than words can reveal.

It happens that love often reveals and is revealed more in what is not said than in what is said. Indeed, our words seldom rise to the love they are meant to confess, to profess, or to share. We know our words are but poor substitutes, doing little more than pointing in the direction of love or limping along after love. We come to see that love is often found among that of which we never speak, among that about which it is better to keep silent. We realize that our words break this silence without making a rent in it.

Lovers of wisdom have little, perhaps nothing, to say of this love. They remain too reserved, too sober to join in the chorus that sings of it. And thus their words are already a skepticism.

There is and can be no *comprehension* of this love *in its concept*. For there is, and can be, no concept of this love. A concept of love necessarily falls short, seeking to capture love or to convey love in some synchronizing generalization. It would substitute the dead letter for the living heart-and-mind. It would attempt to bridge the infinite distance between word and deed. Yet such maneuvers always arrive too late, lingering in winter while it is already spring. And with love it is perennially spring. With love, we commemorate again and again for the first time our being with one another through caring, through meeting, through dwelling. With love, we bring forth again and again for the first time the caring, meeting, and dwelling from which love grows.

The concept is put forth by one who stands outside, a spectator, a by-stander; put forth by one who observes from a distance, seeking to synchronize love in a concept, to dissolve love in a generalization that effaces the different in the same. Such attempts to comprehend love in its concept can only betray love.

Love: Shared, Between Us

The love to which we aspire is shared between us. It is not a sentiment or some feeling of attachment. Nor is it a reflection or extension of paternal benevolence and affection—be it human or divine. It is neither a natural unfolding nor a technical producing; neither a relation of vertical transcendence nor a horizontal fusion. It is not an appropriation, a submission, a reduction of the other to the same, or the subjecting of those who love to the mediating power of some third.

The love shared between us does not presuppose a prior possession, a stockpiling, a hoarding; nor does it presuppose some prior granting or dispensation. Indeed, such economies can lay waste to (our) nature and prevent or impede love between us. It is not the most complete or the most self-sufficient, those who would somehow be closed off and enjoy some private superabundance, who love. It is not those who are already complete(d) who love—but those who are exposed, and in this exposure open with and to others.

The love to which we aspire is a nurturing and cultivating of the caring and sharing through which we dwell, a nurturing and cultivating of our being with one another. It is a love through which we come to dwell in the world anew.

Upon a ground of sharing and caring, we dwell. Upon this ground we can till the field, cultivate the vine, and raise up buildings. Yet our dwelling is not limited to these agri-cultural machinations. Something other and far greater than such intrigues can be brought forth upon this ground. On the ground of sharing and caring, a nurturing and cultivating of our being-with-one-another, of all that lies between us, is also possible—a being-with-one-another not reducible to our coming and going within the field opened and cleared, not reducible to an exchange of goods or of things between us.

Upon the ground of sharing and caring, love too can spring forth, love too can be brought forth. Upon this ground, an accomplished love is possible—not (a) given, but possible. The possibility of such love can be rather difficult to discern when sharing is taken as giving, opening becomes bound, dwelling becomes appropriating, and love is entered as a contract (between symmetrical parties). Upon the ground of sharing and caring, it is indeed the case that giving, closure, appropriation, and contract are possible. The gathering of all beings within a more or less systematic unity is indeed possible upon the ground of sharing and caring. Yet meeting, dwelling, and loving shared between us are also possible.

The love shared between us extends and fecundates our dwelling. And like dwelling, such love is neither given as a gift nor exchanged. It is a love that can only be shared. It is a sharing of heart-and-mind, a sharing in which there might be offering and reception. But even in being received, such love is shared rather than being a simple gift. And even in being offered, such love is shared rather than being simply given.

The love shared between us holds us and supports us—yet it is never to be taken for granted. It slips away in being taken thus. It slips away in being taken as having been dispensed, bestowed from one to another. It slips away in being taken as self-subsisting, as achieved once and for all, as enduring beyond all change. Whatever security or comfort love yields does not accrue to one as a possession or a property, a ground secured for all time. Such love can only be shared through, by, and with an other or others—and only remains insofar as it is *not* retained, held, grasped, appropriated (which is not to say that love is not nurtured and nurturing, supported and supporting).

There is no love greater than a love that is shared. Such love is greater than a love that is merely given—greater even than that love given by some god, greater even than that love that gives life. For the mutual sharing of love is greater than the giving of any gift, greater than the give and take of any goods. Unlike a fountain that forever flows, unlike a cup that never empties, with sharing love grows and grows.

The way of love is open, but who will walk upon it? Who will dwell in this way? The home in which this love dwells is open to all. Nothing is closed off or held back willingly. All is there for the sharing.

Yet if you know not of these things, how can you be persuaded?

Love Conjugated

The love shared between us is a conjugation of our devotion to one another. Thus, we ought not even say: There is a love between us. The love between us is not subordinated to an impersonal being in which it would be some good, even the highest good, to be exchanged, traded back and forth. The love in question here is not an impersonal love. Yet, it is neither mine nor yours. It belongs to no one. Rather, we belong to it.

The love shared between us is not in need of any middle term—a god for instance—that might bridge some supposed chasm between us. Such love is a going on the way together. It is a sharing of breath, of words, of deeds. It is a sharing of bread around a common hearth, a communal table. It is a feast that shares forth love yet again. It is an intertwining of hearts-and-minds, an intertwining of lives in a joint destiny, a commemoration and renewal of the sharing, caring, meeting, and dwelling through which and from out of which our being with one another blossoms and bears fruit.

Our love is a conjugation of our devotion to one another. In such love, we are bound to one another. We draw so close and are drawn so close with those we love that distinctions between inner and outer become difficult to discern— distinctions that are not equivalent to those between self and other. We are not merely open to those we love. Our exposure is much more profound than that. To be open to others implies that we could in principle become closed. But in this love we are so turned inside out that to close would still be to be exposed.

Such love is to be conjugated in the first person plural: We love one another. For this love is not accomplished by one alone. Through and within this shared love, this sharing of love, we can indeed say, "I love (to) you." But love pronounced in this way hearkens back to and calls forth the love shared between us.

Our caring, meeting, and dwelling with one another offer the place and occasion for a love between us. With such love, it is not first and foremost a matter of preference or choice. It is not a matter of selection, but one of *election*. We are with one another, gathered together in advance of any preference, any choice, any *selection*. Whatever preference or choice there may be in such love moves along an incline, an inclining toward, that precedes any preference or choice. Like all our ways of being with one another, loving one another is a way of working through and working out that care between us.

Our love does not grow straightaway and without effort, and yet it is an altogether native and welcome result of the care between us. It is like the fruit and the flower that result from the seed. The seed does not choose the soil in which it grows. This love is not the result of the preferences and choices, of the thoughts and actions of those bound together in love—those who love do not do what they think or what they wish, but what they must. And yet that they must love is no limitation or constraint upon their freedom. Their love is not a fate that compels, but a being-sent-along-the-way-together. In loving they are set free to and for themselves, to and for one another.

Love: Waymaking-With-One-Another

This love is no charity—and the home in which it dwells is no almshouse.

That is to say, such love does not seek to dominate or to make dependent. It does not seek to give to the other what one finds in one's possession. Nor does it seek to bestow upon the other—the height of bestowal already implying at least the threat of dependence or domination.

Rather, such love is a love of the other. It is a love that comes from the other and goes to the other. It is a love shared with the other. If it is *of* the other or *for* the other, it is because it is first *with* the other. With the love shared between us, our love of the other or for the other is a love we share with the other. It is a waymaking with the other; a waymaking with the other that is a waymaking together—sharing with one another, caring with one another, meeting with one another, dwelling with one another.

This waymaking is a going along the way together. It is a wandering together in wonder, a joint opening of and to wonder. Through and within this wonder there can be a disclosure of the possibilities of each one as well as a joint disclosure of shared possibilities. Through and within this wonder, there can be an intertwining of destinies.

Going on the way with one another, it is possible for one to take from the other, for one to give to the other. But such give and take first become possible because we share with the other in a mutual waymaking. On the way together, one can leap in for an other—taking the place of the other, taking over the concerns of the other. And on the way together, one can leap ahead for an other—helping to disclose to the other the other's possibilities—and thereby help the other to become who they are. And, on the way together, there can be a leaping-ahead-together in which shared possibilities are jointly disclosed. Yet our being on the way together is not reducible to leaping-in or leaping-ahead for one another, or even to leaping-ahead-together. Nor is our being on the way together reducible to a disclosure of possibilities, shared or otherwise. For to wander together in wonder exceeds all possibility.

Love: Of the World

Our love is of this world. It is born of this world and dies of this world. It is a humble and limited love. It is not infinite. Nor is it unconditional. It has no power over death. And yet, it *abides*. It sojourns in this world, it dwells in this world, it remains faithful to this world. And in its abiding, it enjoys a certain timelessness. For with love, we fall out of time together—the months and years passing in the blink of an eye. And in the wonder of this moment, here and now, all is perfect, all is redeemed. Nothing is wanting.

The challenge is to extend the opening of this moment so that it envelops the entirety of our lives.

Our love is of this world. That is, with loving we say "Yes!" to the earth. We say "Yes!" to this world, here and now. For in saying "Yes!" here and now, we say "Yes!" to all that is. Our love is a yes-saying, repeated again and again— always for the first time. It is the great liberator and joy-bringer, deeper than any reconciliation.

Love: Of Flesh

Love is deeply rooted in our flesh—rooted more deeply than the giving and taking of a rib would imply, rooted more deeply than any suffering or pain or loss, rooted more deeply than any isolation or loneliness. Those with whom we share this love are born of the same flesh. They are not mere spirit. They are our brothers and our sisters. And we do not dwell far apart. We breathe the same air, drink from the same fountain, share the same fruits of the earth, warm ourselves by the same fire.

In this way, our flesh is already spiritualized. With such love, we touch and are touched. We smell and taste one another. We hear and see one another. With such love all the senses are awakened and each day is a dawning of creation. There is no opposition here between body and soul. Nor is there a reduction of the one to the other. Rather, the body abides in the soul and the soul abides in the body.

Even the most ethereal of loves is rooted in this love of the flesh. Love can only grow up into the thin air of the heavens insofar as it remains rooted in the flesh. A love uprooted from the flesh withers and dies—and there is no being reborn in or of or to some spirit, for that too withers and dies when uprooted from the flesh, in which alone there is life.

Divine Love: Mysterious Love

The love shared between us is a mutual turning toward—that is, a mutual worshiping. And this worshiping is an adoration—that is, a saluting and reverencing of each one, of the mystery of each one, and of the mystery that lies between us. It is a mutual turning toward one another and a mutual turning toward all that lies between us. This turning toward does not seek to obliterate or obscure the mystery of each one or of all that lies between us, but to share in the fecundation of such mystery. It is a turning toward that respects and salutes the mystery of the other, the mystery of each one, the mystery between us.

The mutual turning toward of this love shared between us illuminates the caring, meeting, and dwelling we share. All that extends and is shared between us sparkles and shines in the luminosity of this love. And each one sparkles and shines in the luminosity of this love.

Such love is ecstatic. But this ecstasy does not consist in being driven out of one's senses. Rather, through our love with one another, we are beside ourselves. We are touched by the mystery of the other, we are enveloped in the mystery of the other, we share in the mystery of the other. And we become seers and wise to the verge of madness. Our lives are transformed and translated through our love with one another. We are moved beyond ourselves.

The love shared between us is a love of the divine, of the divine between us, of the divine that together we become and are. Such love brings forth gods and goddesses; through and within such love we become gods and goddesses ourselves.

You will never be closer to any god than you are right now. Yet you cannot be made to see this. You cannot be made to share in love.

Transformative Love

The love shared between us leaves nothing untouched. It leaves nothing as it was before. Through and within our loving one another, we are completed and made whole—not by becoming closed off and securing some stasis, but by being placed fully and harmoniously within the swaying movement of all-that-is.

We become complete, we become whole through caring with and for others, through meeting with others, through dwelling with others. Which is to say that we become whole together. We are not separate and self-sufficient entities. Our being is always being-with. And our being-well is a being-well-with-one-another. We do not and cannot become whole, become complete by ourselves, through self-exertion, through self-effort. No matter how important such exertion or effort may be, they do not suffice. The well-being of each and all is firmly tied together. And if our exertions or efforts close us off in a supposed self-sufficiency, they can lead us away from the way of love and away from our well-being.

The love shared between us is the good (beyond being) that, together, we seek. It is that for the sake of which we live. Loving is our being-well-with-one-another. It is caring well, meeting well, dwelling well with one another. The love shared between us is a singular and precious jewel; a crowning glory of the caring, meeting, and dwelling shared between us. It is an end and acme of our sharing, caring, meeting, and dwelling with one another—an end and acme that transforms all our ways of being-with-one-another.

The Swaying Movement of All That Is

And still season follows upon season, and nothing dies forever. Again and again the earth shares forth myriad things. And light follows upon dark, the warm upon the cold, the moist upon the dry, and life follows upon death. Each shares with each, coming together and pulling apart. Each shares with each—arising together, coming together, departing together. The knot of existence so firmly tied together in and through this sharing that none stands apart from the others.